MOTORCYCLES

Weidenfeld & Nicolson London

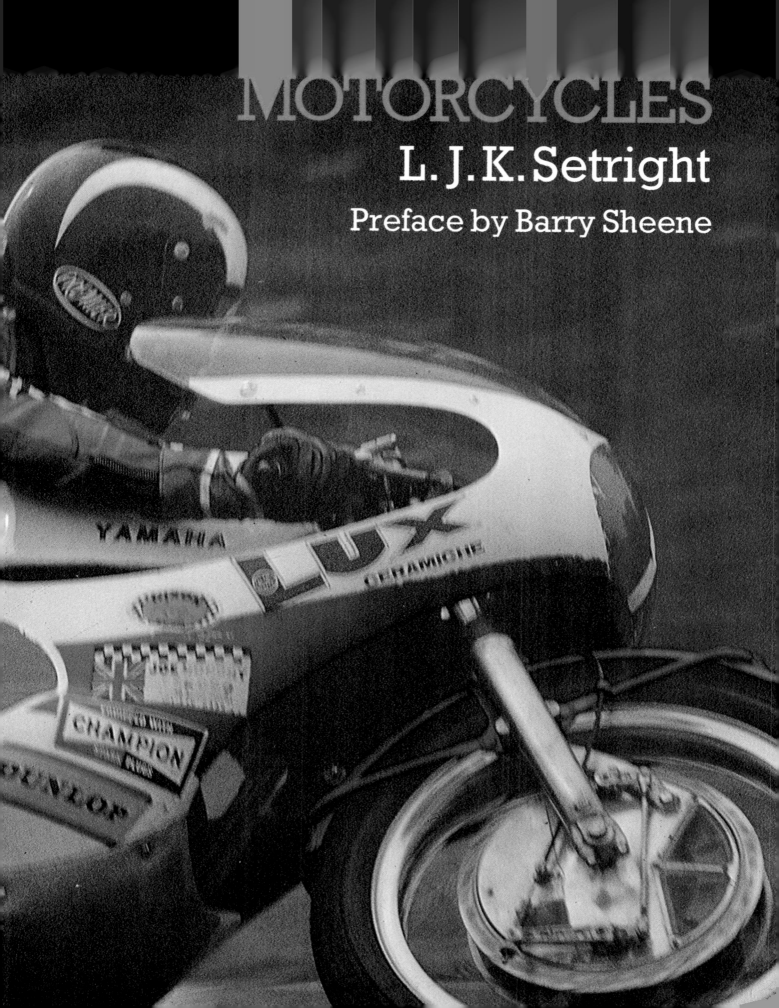

MOTORCYCLES

L. J. K. Setright

Preface by Barry Sheene

Art director Behram Kapadia
Designed by Gill Mouqué
for George Weidenfeld and Nicolson Ltd
11 St John's Hill, London SW11

House editor Esther Jagger

ISBN 0 297 77234 1

Filmset by Keyspools Limited, Golborne, Lancs.

Printed in Great Britain by Morrison & Gibb Limited,
Edinburgh.

Contents

Barry Sheene, one of the most popular and well-known riders on the international circuit, has been leader of the Suzuki works team for four years.

Preface
by Barry Sheene

Motorcycles have always fascinated me. I was brought up in a motorcycle racing environment because my father, Frank Sheene, not only raced himself but also worked on other people's racing engines. As long ago as I can remember there were engines and parts of engines in my father's workshop, a place that quickly became a major attraction for me. When I was five I was given my first machine, a 49 cc four-stroke Ducati, but it was not just riding that interested me. I wanted to know how it worked, too.

By the age of fifteen I was actually working on other people's racing engines. I left school at the first opportunity and my first job, just before my sixteenth birthday, was as mechanic for an American road racer, Tony Woodman, who was racing in Europe. It was up to me to look after 350 cc AJS 7R and 500 cc G50 Matchless engines, and best of all I was involved with Grand Prix racing. Of course at that time I never imagined that one day I would earn my living as a motorcycle road racer.

But it is not just the racing that interests and excites me. The sight of any eye-catching or technically intriguing machine, whether competition or road-going, has always aroused my curiosity – and until I have actually had a go on it myself I am not satisfied.

The sad fact that becomes obvious as the history of the motorcycle unfolds is that the British industry, so often the leader in design and technology, is nearing extinction. If only it had realized ten years ago that the future lay in two-stroke machines – for a lengthy spell anyway – it would still be going strong now.

For me the biggest step forward in years was the Ariel Leader, and the Ariel Arrow that followed. It was a winner on the road, and with a little development it was a winner on the race track, too. The twin-cylinder, two-stroke engine may have given problems, and unchanged it certainly would not challenge modern strokers, but if development had continued the Japanese industry would have had a fight on its hands to compete and certainly would not have the monopoly it enjoys today. The Ariel Leader surely had just what the average road rider wants – weather protection, a good range of power, and adequate handling.

The only British bikes I can claim to have owned are a Triumph Tiger Cub and a BSA Bantam, and neither of those comes into the exotic bracket. The Triumph came after the Ducati, while the Bantam, tuned by my father, was just about the fastest machine of its kind around London in the mid-sixties, when for a time I delivered proofs for an advertising agency. Between the Triumph and the BSA I owned a Bultaco Sherpa trials bike, and with it got my first taste of real competition.

Although not a superbike, I feel that the Bantam really deserves a mention in a parade of motorcycles that matter and that have played a part in the evolution of the breed. It was a winner in its time, providing cheap transport of a reliable nature, which is perhaps the most important factor for the everyday motorcyclist. Who knows – in a modern guise the Bantam could still be a winner. On the sporting side I am amazed at the performance of its single-cylinder, two-stroke engine which, even now, years after it went out of production, provides competitive racing for clubmen and enthusiasts of the marque.

After the Bantam I went Japanese with a 250 Suzuki – the manufacturer to whom I have been under contract for racing for almost four years. Although racing now takes up most of my motorcycle-riding time I still enjoy the exhilaration of riding my Suzuki GT750 on the road. The one machine I have actually owned in the line-up of stars that follows is the Suzuki RE5. The obvious mechanical attraction of the first big production Wankel-engined machine made me want to have one. It is an ideal touring bike, a top-gear roller.

Leonard Setright has embarked on a man-sized task in bringing together a collection of machines that mark important and memorable steps on the ladder of two-wheeler design and development. His book is an ideal cross-section of what has gone on in the world of motorcycles over the last seventy years. It is an excellent record of what has brought success, heartbreak and big hopes for the future.

Prologue

In the eighty or more years since the first steps were taken to put motorized bicycles into production, over two thousand brands of motorcycles have been produced in at least thirty countries. The great majority of them have been anything but memorable; but this is a book about motorcycles that have mattered. Many were machines of some technical merit, or of great commercial moment; all will, I believe, be seen as significant by historians – though if that were the sole criterion for determining the list there would be some others demanding inclusion, such as the Harley Davidson monsters, an unholy rabble of European pipsqueaks, and – most promising and disappointing of all – the Ariel Leader.

Historical significance, as it happens, is not all that matters. To chronicle evolution, of which we have seen much, and revolution of which there has been sadly little, might merely have tempted me to write the text of this book as though to pillory the manufacturers who have spent the last seven decades so stubbornly doing the wrong thing, and to upbraid the public for always supposing that it was the right thing. Yet this would not be proper; the enthusiastic motorcyclist gets more out of his machine than the technologists could ever put into it.

Motorcycling is more than a matter of stresses and strains, of thermodynamic and gyroscopic cycles and precessions. It demands emotional involvement as well as physical; it puts more premium on spirit than on substance; it is a means to heighten one's awareness of environment while yet escaping from its pressures. Because it is something that should be undertaken from choice rather than from necessity, it must be a sport even to the least competitive rider; and it is therefore entitled to its traditions, its assumptions and its perversities, however ill-founded, irrational or indefensible they may be. One cannot compound religion with a slide rule.

Neither can one capture the essence of adventure in a table of specifications. Detailed technical analyses would be out of place in a story where the subliminal theme is of romance – and these are motorcycles with strong romantic associations, here for the deeds they accomplished, the legends they founded, or the trends they demonstrated by their successes or failures. Not all of them were made in large quantities, nor were they all famous. Some were pathetically misunderstood, and failed to become the money-making successes they should have been; others were cunningly devised to deceive, and were a lot more successful than they deserved. Some won races, others lost them; all were important.

LJKS
April 1976

Art nouveau: one of the tiled pictures by Gilardoni Fils, *c.* 1910, decorating the Michelin building in London shows the Frenchman Bucquet riding the New Werner to victory in the 1902 race from Paris to Vienna.

New Werner

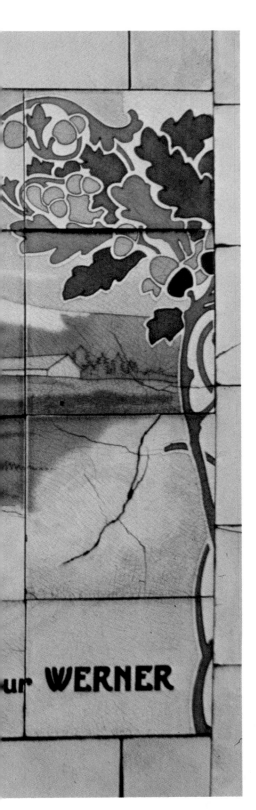

ur WERNER

But is a motorcycle a practical touring machine? Excellent as it is for excursions, I am afraid not; . . . but is the machine practical? Is it a rival to the ordinary cycle for touring? I think not . . .

But is the system right? I am afraid not for touring. I do not in this matter refer to the Werner especially, which seems to me to be the only motorcycle at all practical; all the others I have seen have some fatal or absurd defect. But can a motor, of say one or two horsepower, be attached to a bicycle; can the bicycle be made strong enough to stand the strain? And, if so, is it safe to ride, over all sorts of roads and under all sorts of conditions? I regret to say, I am afraid not. . . . But, if the strength is obtained, is it safe to ride from 12 to 25 miles an hour up hill and down hill, on dry and wet roads, and through traffic? Though it is most fascinating, I believe it is equally dangerous.

Thus wrote the artist and author Mr Jo Pennell after essaying a short tour of France on a Werner motor bicycle. It was not the archetypal New Werner, but one of the earlier front-drive types. Its frame was that of a current 'new safety bicycle' and its design featured a single-cylinder engine mounted in front of the steering head, the power being transmitted from its crankshaft to its front wheel by way of a belt of twisted rawhide running over grooved pulleys. Indeed it was the brothers Werner, French in nationality though Russian in origin, who had reintroduced this belt drive which Daimler had pioneered considerably earlier, relying on it to eliminate all the problems of harshness and intractability characteristic of most of the early motorcycles with their inflexible engines and unyielding transmissions. We may not necessarily accept Mr Pennell's verdict that the Werner was superior to all its contemporaries; but since it shared with them the one basic absurd and potentially fatal defect – that it constituted nothing more than a conventional pedal bicycle to which an engine had been clipped on by some mechanically unsympathetic and dynamically perilous means – we can share all his misgivings about the practicality, the safety and even the desirability of these machines. We can go further and endorse his verdict that motorcycling, even with the aid of such machines leaving so much to be desired, could be most fascinating.

It was this legacy of the pedal cycle, from which the motorcycle industry has not yet shaken itself free, that made those pioneers so unsatisfactory. Frame breakages were not uncommon; and when (as was often the case) they took place in the unsprung front forks, the consequences could be painful or even deadly. The superimposition of an effective but crude and vibratory engine upon this scarcely suitable frame aggravated all the handling deficiencies attributable to a high centre of gravity, a short wheelbase, and tyres of tenuous proportions and inadequate grip.

Locations for the engine varied in those days from the inconvenient to the ludicrous: they might be attached to either front or rear hub, ahead of the machine or behind it, above or below the bottom bracket, within the plane of the wheels or without – and despite the evident popularity of the front-wheel-drive Werner, the driven wheel was more likely to be the rear. Certainly as popular as the Werner was the Belgian Minerva, whose layout involved a belt drive to the rear wheel from a sloping engine slung beneath the front down-tube of the bicycle frame; and this was a layout widely copied, whether with the aid of engines and fittings purchased from the Minerva company or with designs which had, as was frequently the case with the plethora of engines of the De Dion type, been pirated.

At least the engine location of the Minerva encouraged further steps in the right direction. It is only fair, however, to draw attention to the particularly neat little machine built by one George Gibson of Birkenhead, who in 1900 designed a machine whose crankcase replaced the conventional bottom bracket, its crankshaft being coaxial with the pedal axis, and its sloping single cylinder replacing the lower portion of the front down-tube. This was a design far more elegant than any of its contemporaries, anticipating the sloper designs of the Yorkshireman Josiah Phelon and his many later imitators. It was just a little unfortunate that the transmission of engine power to the rear wheel should have been by chain without any form of cushioning or spring drive: there was nothing about the Gibson $1\frac{3}{4}$ horsepower engine that would absolve it from the allegations of harshness that could properly be levelled at all engines of the period, and this intransigent transmission must have been responsible for the commercial failure of what otherwise seemed a singularly well-balanced and robust design. This was no 'clip-on', as the popular expression of the day described contem-

BELOW The Werner stand in the 1905 Paris Salon.

ABOVE Until the Werner integration of engine with frame spread to most motorcycles, the most practical of alternative layouts was this one, popularized by Minerva.

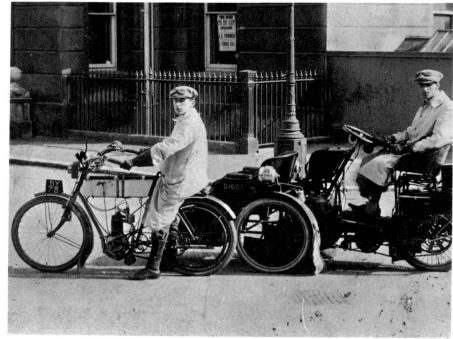

RIGHT By about 1905, the new 'Werner position' for motorcycle engines was generally accepted, though still a matter for comment on the back of this postcard scene. The unidentified bicycle may be an NSU; the tricar is best forgotten, as its genre soon was.

porary machines, but a true motorbicycle.

One year later it was the brothers Werner who hit upon this engine location as the solution to so many of the motorcycling problems of the day. They too produced a machine in which the engine was incorporated into the frame rather than being merely added to it; and although their means of integrating the engine into the frame were much less elegant than Gibson's, they made fewer demands on the structural integrity of the engine itself, and were at least practical. They also made it possible to retain a bracket and spindle for the pedals that were still necessary; and their design embodied a number of other new features including a foot-operated rear brake, while in the engine department a spray carburettor gave better controllability than had the surface carburettors previously common. Another refinement was hand-pump lubrication, absolving the driver from the need to dismount every ten or fifteen miles to administer fresh oil from the can which had formerly to be carried tied onto the machine somewhere.

The great thing about the New Werner, as this machine was soon christened, was that it freed the motorcycle of all the crippling inconveniences that had made earlier machines (including the old Werner) appear to the public as mere freaks, whereas the public had already come to accept the powered tricycle as a practical proposition. With its new-found stability, rigidity, performance and safety, the New Werner provided an archetype for the modern motorcycle, the crystalline form that was to be multiplied and mirrored a thousand times as motorcycles entered upon a decade of emancipation, a decade in which they passed from being experimental playthings of a lunatic minority to becoming the recreational or workaday transport of a considerable number. Within a couple of years the Werner had established itself firmly on the market, aided by a number of competition successes in 1902, the most notable of these being perhaps its victory in the race from Paris to Vienna. It would be overstating the case for the New Werner to suggest that it made such an undertaking as this race between the capitals easy – its French rider, Bucquet, must have been a valiant man indeed – but at least it made the journey feasible.

BELOW LEFT Coming events cast their shadows: in 1904 Werner built a vertical twin.

BELOW In 1903 Minerva still clung to their frame conventions, but in that same year some of their engines had mechanically operated overhead inlet valves.

How many such Isle of Man scenes have we seen? A crate of Wakefield's racing oil, Castrol R; a group of men sharing a problem; and, in this case, a Rudge Multi.

Rudge Multi

In *The Fairies* William Allingham wrote a celebrated quatrain:

> *Up the airy mountain*
> *Down the rushy glen*
> *We daren't go a-hunting*
> *For fear of little men*

Motorcyclists taking part in the Isle of Man Tourist Trophy races twenty-two years after Allingham's death knew exactly what he meant. In 1911 the modest triangular circuit based at St Johns was abandoned for what had already become known in car racing circles as 'the four-inch course' but became immortalized in the motorcyclist's vocabulary as the Mountain Circuit, a $37\frac{3}{4}$-mile tour winding through more than 200 bends up, down, and around

the airy and not infrequently misty sides of Snaefell. The single-geared motor-cycle whose transmission ratio had been calculated to suit the giddy downhill rush to Glen Vine corner would find itself at a considerable disadvantage when climbing the Mountain, and vice versa. In either extreme, especially in the old days of low-grade petrol, the notorious 'little men with hammers' might make their presence felt in the engine. A multi-speed transmission was the obvious solution, but already motorcyclists were proving themselves a conservative – not to say reactionary – kind of people, and having once grown accustomed to single-speed belt-and-pulley transmission they were not easily weaned away from it.

The problems of intractability had for some time been apparent in the single-speed motorcycles of the preceding decade, for a machine that called for such vigorous exertion when starting, stopping, climbing hills, or negotiating tight corners, could never hope to achieve that degree of popularity essential to commercial success. Already in 1905 experiments had been made with a view to providing a range of transmission ratios, stepless or otherwise. Before 1911, two-speed transmissions had appeared in Werner, De Dion Bouton, NSU,

The Rudge is the same one, but the smiles suggest that the problem has gone – or did the lady's company make the difference?

OVERLEAF In 1911 the Rudge Multi was literally a ten days' wonder; by 1920, as here, not enough had changed.

Killed in the IOM in 1911, Victor
Surridge on a Rudge Multi.

Fafnir, Phelon & Moore, Scott, and Enfield, while Chater Lea had introduced a three-speed gearbox as early as 1906.

Still the belt-wielders protested that what they wanted was some form of adjustable pulley, ideally on the engine crankshaft, whose controllable variation in size would provide a simple alteration of the transmission ratio; and various systems were evolved which permitted such adjustments to be carried out while the motorcycle was in motion. In 1911, none of them appeared wholly satisfactory when seen in the light of the strenuous demands likely to be made by the new Mountain Course in the Isle of Man, and the Rudge Whitworth Company felt compelled to devise something better for the benefit of several private owners of belt-driven Rudges who proposed to take part in the TT race.

Rudge Whitworth in fact left it rather late to deal with the problem; but at the last moment inspiration came to them, and during one June week they produced a variable-speed belt drive that was to become immortal. The pulley on the engine shaft was variable in effective diameter, as before, but so was the larger pulley or belt rim on the rear wheel, the idea being that one should expand while the other contracted, so as to maintain constant belt tension over a steplessly variable range of 1.73 : 1. A long lever alongside the fuel tank gave the rider control over the clumsy-looking apparatus which worked well enough for it to earn Rudge Whitworth a large number of sales of the Multi in the years that followed. It was 1914 before a Rudge Multi actually won a TT race, C.G. Pullin riding one in the Senior event that year to average 49.49 miles per hour over the 225-mile course, thus establishing a race average for the Mountain Circuit that was for entirely non-technical reasons to remain a record for six years. . . .

RIGHT Belt troubles killed the Rudge Multi as surely as they did the clumsier Zenith Gradua. Zenith continued to specialize in v-twin load-haulers: this one, with fashionable octagonal aluminium sidecar, carried an East End Pearly King and his family to Epsom Downs for the 1933 Derby.

Indian

The reason for American vowels sounding so sinister is that they are intimately associated with what can be called the 'AEIOU' foreign policy of their speakers: *Americae est imperare orbi universo*. There was a time, prior to the Great War, when the world of motorcycling might well have been dominated by American manufacturers who were growing and multiplying at an impressive rate, and developing a technology that threatened to nullify the early lead taken by the European pioneers. Even in America, you can never rely on anything: along comes a politician (defined by Wallace Stevens as 'A statesman who approaches every question with an open mouth') promising a chicken in every cooker and a car in every garage, and the entire American nation takes him at his word. Although the American motorcycle was then the most advanced, the most sophisticated and at times apparently (albeit not truthfully) the most competent at high speeds of all the world's, the Americans found they could buy mass-

3½ hp Indian of 1911.

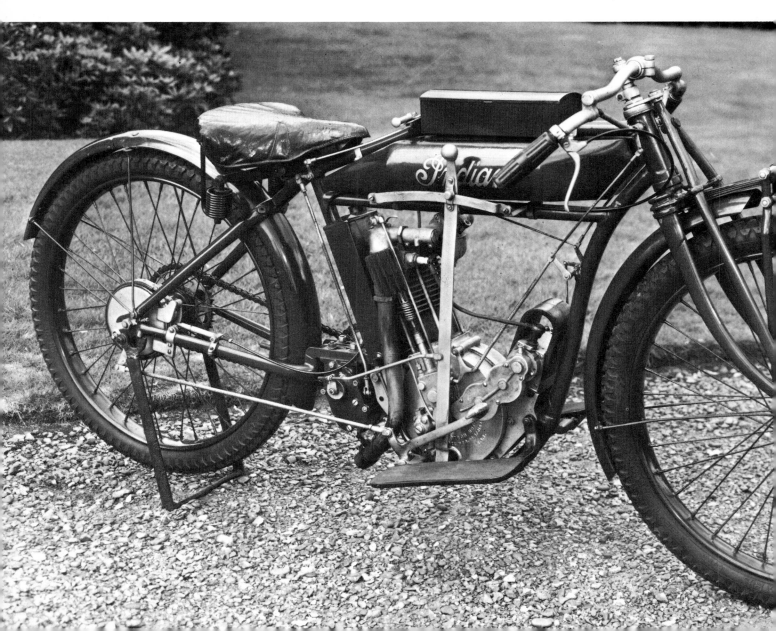

produced cheap cars, and the indigenous motorcycle industry was stopped dead. Like the chicken, it continued to twitch after the mortal blow had been struck, but it was definitely dead from the neck up.

This was a pity, for some of the American manufacturers had some clever engineers, of whom perhaps the most notable was Oscar Hedstrom of the Hendee Manufacturing Company, of Springfield, Massachusetts. Hendee produced the Indian, the leading brand in the USA, and by 1914 the best-selling foreigner on the British market; and under Hedstrom's direction, Indian motorcycles took a clear lead in technical developments.

George Hendee started work with Hedstrom in 1900, the company being established in the following year. At first they used a proprietary Thor engine, but they were quick to impress their own ideas on the still malleable motorcycle: they did away with the saddle-tube that was a normally constituent part of the basic bicycle frame, and in its place set the single-cylinder engine. By 1904 a twistgrip had taken the place of the clumsy throttle levers to which many European riders would be condemned for decades to come; a year later, the original backward sloping cylinder was given the company of a forward sloper

Victorious Indian rider Oliver C. Godfrey in the paddock after the 1911 Senior TT. To his right, the vanquished Matchless director Charlie Collier, whose brother Harry is in the background.

ABOVE Wearing armband 16 is the
American Teddy K. Hastings who came
to Britain to ride this 4 hp Indian in the
1907 1000-mile trial. Competing on a
Vindec was W. H. Wells (far right) who
was to become the foremost importer of
Indians.

RIGHT Billy Wells escorts Indian rider
O. C. Godfrey from the winner's
rostrum after the 1911 Senior TT.

ahead of it, making the engine a v-twin of about half a litre displacement. By 1908 the inlet valves were cam-operated instead of being left to flutter open and shut according to pressure gradients across their ports; and by 1914, Indians had electric lighting and even electric starting. It was proper that an American motorcycle should be the first to feature these facilities, for it was an American car, the Cadillac, that was the first to do likewise on four wheels, thanks to the perfectionist Henry Leland and the inventive Charles Kettering. Even Rolls-Royce were not to make such electrical equipment standard until 1919, nor would it reappear in motorcycles until Honda got busy on the problem forty years later – though George Brough shoe-horned a starter motor into a one-off specially adapted for a disabled customer in the 1920s.

Nor was it only their modern conveniences that made these early Indians such desirable properties. They were fairly manageable by the standards of their times, despite such unusual features as the footboards which took the place of conventional pedals, and the passing of which is still lamented by riders who have tried them. Moreover the Indians were fast, and capable of being made to go very fast indeed. Long before an Indian set the first official world speed record at 103.5 mph in 1920, the firm had successfully attacked all existing distance records from 1 to 100 miles. To hammer the lesson home in Europe, where the market was getting better all the time, they sent a single-cylinder Indian to break the 1-hour class record at Brooklands in 1911, and followed it with a team of specially built v-twins for the Senior TT that was to be run for the first time over the Mountain Course that year.

They attracted considerable praise, not only for their basic design but also for the clever adaptations made to suit the needs of high-speed riding on give-and-take roads. The lever controlling the two-speed gearbox, on the right of the petrol tank, was moved forward so that a rider could work it easily while in a racing crouch, doing rapid clutchless gear changes because the throttle was

25

controlled by the *left* twistgrip – the one on the right controlled ignition advance and the valve lifters that aided starting. If the clutch were needed, there was a lever on the left of the tank that could be set to give any desired slip – a rather nasty device, but similar in function to the rocking clutch pedal that was normal on road-going Indians.

The team of four v-twins, with overhead inlet and side exhaust valves, leaf-sprung front forks and open exhausts, dominated the 1911 Senior TT. They certainly did not have things all their own way, but they rocked the establishment by finishing first, second and third. The British had to console themselves with the thought that the Indians had very nearly been beaten by their favourite Charles Collier, on a single-cylinder Matchless, who was leading at the half-way stage when a puncture dropped him to third place; after fighting his way back to second, he was disqualified for refuelling away from the official depots. As for the honour of the day's fastest lap, this fell to Frank Philipp, a relation of Alfred Scott, who was riding the new and fascinating rotary-valve Scott two-stroke that was to win in the following year.

The British public, and to some extent the Continentals, were to remain impressed by the speed of the Springfield Fliers for many years to come; but in America things were changing too rapidly for the motorcycle manufacturers to retain control of their destinies. Immediately after the Great War, Indian brought out some new models that should have been of guaranteed popularity: and in fact the 596 cc side-valve Indian Scout v-twin was one of their most favoured products, enduring with improvements for a very long time after its introduction in 1919. Alas, George Hendee left the company during the late 1920s and control passed into the hands of men who seemed to lack experience, judgment, or foresight. Perhaps Indian did very well to keep going as long as they did: within years of the American motorcar industry flooding the market with amazingly cheap mass-produced transport, the prolific American motorcycle industry had been reduced to two firms – Harley Davidson, who were better managed and survived, and Indian, who somehow kept going on police and military work until the early 1950s.

ABOVE LEFT After George Hendee left the firm he had created, Indian went some strange ways. In 1927 they took over the 1265 cm^3 ACE in-line four, which became the Indian-4 in 1929 and remained on the scene until 1941.

ABOVE The Indian Forty-Five (its cubic inches equalling 744 cm^3) sprang from the Police Scout of the late 1920s: a spring frame was a late concession to advancing years before Indian's American production ceased in 1953.

The American motorcycle, which had once promised so much future brilliance, decayed because when it needed enthusiasm and engineers all it got was indifference, insularity and inbreeding. Designs became so repetitious, so unimaginative, so gross and impractical, and from a strict engineering standpoint so unforgivably inept, that the standard American motorcycle of which the Indian represented the norm became an object of derision. Soldiers and speed-cops had to put up with it, because there was not the faintest hope of being issued with anything better from overseas; but if we draw a merciful curtain over the last failing decades of the firm, we might allow ourselves to peep through a chink at this quotation from an instruction manual issued to motorcycle patrolmen of the New York Police Department: 'The motorcycle itself is a very tricky and hazardous machine to operate and must be thoroughly understood by the operator before he attempts to operate it. Therefore, he must at all times handle it with care and caution. When handled carelessly or negligently it will trick the rider, care and caution are the best policy in dealing with the vehicle.'

Scott

Yorkshiremen seem to have a special part in the history of the motorcycle. Alfred Scott did even better: he had a special role even among Yorkshiremen and among motorcyclists. His followers sometimes mistakenly supposed him to have shared this obsession with his best known work, but in fact he was a man of extremely fertile imagination and indeed of broader interests than might be found among many of the ruder forefathers of the industry. What other designer of note ever kept a grand piano alongside his drawing board for recreation? It was right, and proper, that the Scott motorcycle was like nothing else; and when it was pilloried for its individuality, its agile-brained progenitor was quick to turn the pillories into a hustings.

Late in 1908 the newly aggrandized Auto-Cycle Union issued an edict governing the eligibility of two-stroke-engined motorcycles in competition. All aircooled two-strokes, it said, should have their capacities multiplied by a factor of 1.25 in order to make for fairer terms of competition with the conventional four-strokes which fired only half as often. For water-cooled two-strokes the factor should be 1.32. The edict was accepted with relief by most of the motorcycle industry; and it was broadcast with relish in the publicity material put out by Alfred Scott, the manufacturer of the only water-cooled two-stroke.

He maintained that the ruling had been issued solely in order to handicap the machines he produced, and of course he was right: having entered his beautiful new two-stroke twin for the Wass Bank hillclimb in July 1908, when he put up the best performance to win the Dyson Shield and the gold medal, he had then gone on to the Newnham event in the following month to win the open twin-cylinder and variable-gear classes and three gold medals. The rest of the trade retired hurt to commence their lobbying of the ACU; but in the long run it made no difference, for the two-stroke that Scott so brilliantly pioneered was to remain with us. His own basic design has endured for sixty years, while other more sophisticated two-strokes abound on the world's roads and dominate the smaller classes on the world's racing circuits, often exploiting rotary valves that are a development of those devised by Scott for his successful racing machines of 1912 to 1914.

Those special Scotts won the Senior Tourist Trophy races of 1912 and 1913, but for the motorcyclist who looked for more practical demonstrations of the road-going virtues and was unimpressed by arbitrary capacity classification, Scott could perform other feats. There was for example the matter of 100 consecutive climbs and descents of Sutton Bank, a majestic Yorkshire hill with a gradient averaging 1 in 8 and sections which in 1911 were twice as steep. Clearly the simple three-port crankcase-compression two-stroke engine to which Scott had been addicted since 1898 was now, as a result of his attention, capable of sustaining maximum effort for long periods, while its mechanical simplicity and operational flexibility did a great deal more to endear it to the long-suffering riders of the time. The pickaxe voice of the Scott as it began to break down the opposition also grew into a legend, as did the other virtues of the machine.

ABOVE On his way to second place in the 1924 Senior TT, Harry Langman riding the Scott with which he was always associated. He started nine TTs on this make, but 1924 yielded his best result.

RIGHT Two-speed 496 cm³ Scott of 1924 at a VMCC rally in 1967.

FAR RIGHT The open-frame two-speeder in 1922 TT trim, and Harry Langman again.

28

ABOVE Low centre of gravity, triangulated frame, linear front suspension travel and that redoubtable water-cooled two-stroke twin: all the main Scott features are present in this 1923 model.

RIGHT It looks just as unusual and as convincing from this angle . . .

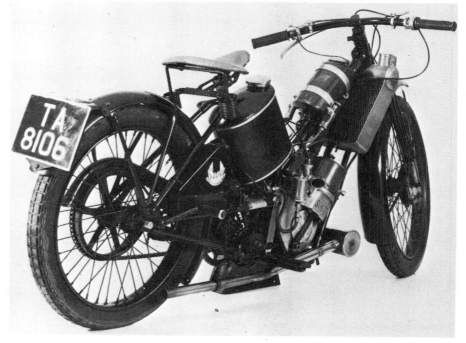

People likened the yowl of its exhaust to the sound of a giant ripping huge sheets of calico. Compared with later racing two-strokes, notably the supercharged DKW of the late 1930s, the sound of the Scott might more resemble the gentle unravelling of a piece of knitting; but in 1939, as thirty years earlier or for that matter thirty years later, the protagonists of the Scott were rationally and emotionally convinced that the virtues of the make were inimitable and indispensable.

The tenets of this faith were established when Scott, investigating in 1898 the possibilities of a general utility power unit, produced a two-stroke with two parallel aircooled cylinders whose pistons were connected to overhung crankpins set 180° apart on a shaft with a substantial central flywheel to minimize the rocking couple that can adversely affect the otherwise extreme smoothness of an engine so disposed. Already he saw the need for the crankcase volume to be minimized in the interests of volumetric efficiency, and he saw also the tremendous scope which such an engine offered for motorcycling. When he was not using it to drive a small boat he would fit the engine to a pedal cycle whose front wheel it drove by a friction roller. Then in 1903 he built a slightly larger engine (with dual ignition) which was attached to the steering head of a bicycle frame but now drove the rear wheel by a belt-coupled friction pulley.

His prototype engine sufficiently proven, Scott then turned his attention to frame design. In this, too, he demonstrated his contempt for the commercial equivocations and engineering incompetence of his contemporaries in the motorcycle industry, concentrating instead on the intelligent and original application of sound mechanical principles to produce a frame almost completely triangulated, stiffer in beam strength and much stiffer in torsion than any other. For his front forks he satisfied himself at this early stage, as the rest of the industry were to do thirty or forty years later, that the straight-line motion of telescopic fork legs was most desirable – while contriving, as most of them had yet to do, to produce a design free from the dangers of asymmetrical loading or springing. This he did by modifying the existing Rex type forks whose tubular blades slid in guides to give the desired geometry of motion, simplifying them by the adoption of a single central spring unit at the top of the fork, and in front of the steering head.

The transmission he may have modelled upon the two-speed transmission used in 1906 by his fellow Yorkshireman Josiah Phelon, comprising a pair of primary chains running on sprockets of different sizes individually keyed or dog-clutched onto a countershaft from which the secondary chain drove the back wheel. Phelon, despite the anger he expressed at the time, was not the first to use it, as Scott made clear in his defence to his rival's lawsuit.

Nor was Scott the first gifted engineer to lack the capital with which to back his projects. Accordingly he contracted the Bradford brothers Willy and Ben Jowett to manufacture his design, which they began in 1908. As first conceived, it was of 450 cm³ capacity, having aircooled cylinder barrels and a water-cooled cylinder head piped into a thermosyphonic circuit with a radiator mounted immediately above – a radiator whose tubular header tank was to become one of the distinguishing marks of the Scott for ever after. However, the Jowetts had other projects, and handed back the Scott contract in 1909: so with a shoestring or two the Scott Company and factory were established. The motorcycles it produced earned enormous popularity, and when Scott retired from the company in 1919 (he died in 1923 aged 49 years) it was said he sold out for £52,000 – more than thirty-two times his original 1909 shareholding.

The customers whom this money ultimately represented were on the whole well pleased with their purchases. The Scott two-speeder offered a unique amalgam of the features that a discriminating rider sought. Its steering and handling were generally considered superlative in those days, thanks principally to the stiffness of the frame and the low centre of gravity it permitted, though the steering geometry itself must have made a worthwhile contribution. As for the engine, it was the paragon of sweetness and reliability in an age when most others were vicious in their manners and precarious in their fallibility. The water cooling must have made a worthwhile contribution to this, being extended to include the cylinders in 1911; for in those days of poor-quality fuel, imperfect carburation, and incomplete knowledge, air cooling was never wholly satisfactory, as the aero-engine manufacturers continued to find throughout the 1914–18 war. Yet Scott's genius contrived further advantages, the design of the engine making it fantastically easy to work on: the big-end bearings, for example, could be removed and replaced by the roadside in a matter of minutes.

Another change in 1911 was to increase the swept volume to 532.5 cm³. It was a curious figure, and for a touring machine it was perhaps irrelevant; but the capacity classes by which the sport was governed had by now impressed themselves on the minds of ordinary customers, and when this classic machine was reintroduced in 1920, and given the name Squirrel, its bore and stroke were set at 70 and 63.5mm respectively to bring the capacity down to 486 cm³, within the conventional half-litre limit. In this form it developed about 14 bhp at 3200 rpm, sufficient to give a very lively performance to a machine which weighed less than 200 lb. To some extent its performance might be hampered

... and the essentials were there by 1910.

32

by the availability of but two alternative ratios in its transmission: in the interests of the acceleration and hillclimbing for which the Scott was justly famous, these were standardized at 3.75 and 5.4 to 1, allowing a maximum speed of more than 60 mph.

The more modern three-speed Scott featured the 'long' tank, filling the open frame, that had become a four-guinea option on the two-speeder in 1926.

This was not enough to permit serious competition with the racing four-strokes of the day, delightful though the Scott remained as a road or cross-country machine; and although that devoted Scott rider Harry Langman averaged 56.09 mph in the 1922 Senior TT, it only brought him third place behind the 58.31 mph winning Sunbeam. It was the same story in the 1923 Manx GP, the first-ever TT for amateurs, in which the best Scott finished eighth at 47.13 and the winning Sunbeam at 52.77. Thereafter the Scott was never a force to be reckoned with in racing, but the lovely little open-framed two-speeder continued to be the repository of many a rider's faith for practically a decade, gradually being supplanted by the 'New' Scott, the closed-frame three-speed Flying Squirrel which came on the market in 1927 after its racing debut in 1926.

There were those who said that it did not steer as well as the old one, but fundamentally it was still the same design. In the years after the World War little difference could be seen except in the suspension, and when the company folded up the motorcycle still remained available, built to special order by devotee Martin Holder in Birmingham – alas that it could not be in Yorkshire – throughout the 1960s and even beyond. By that time another devotee, George Silk, was doing wonders with a vintage Scott in club events and gradually the machine was developed and modified until none of it was Scott; yet the resemblance remains, and the modern, elegant and behaviourally exemplary Silk is as much like a Scott as anything ever was. There are those that say the modern Scott fanatic is championing a lost cause; but in his play *The Dark is Light Enough* the poet Christopher Fry provides the answer: 'I know your cause is lost; but in the heart of all right causes is a cause that cannot lose.'

33

Brough Superior SS100

Late in 1934 the SS80 was supplemented by an 80 Special with an AMC engine replacing the old JAP – and of course with handsome valve-chests bearing the name Brough Superior. The same 750 cm³ side-valver powered the 1937 transverse twin.

INSET Evidence of the essential durability of the SS100 appears in the background here; a BSA Gold Star c. 1960.

Can the whole be greater than the sum of its parts? In cooking and counterpoint and collage it can; but it is rare to find in motorcycles any such defiance of the logician's syllogistic strictures. The Brough Superior was such a rare motorcycle: rare because it was undoubtedly invested with a glamour, a mystique, even a kind of nobility, beyond any expectations that a study of its specification might prompt; and rare because, in the twenty years that George Brough devoted to motorcycle manufacture, he produced little more than 3000 specimens, an output that in modern times might be matched by BMW in five months and by Honda in fewer days. Perhaps, then, George Brough was an artist – a collage artist, taking bits and pieces from this source and that, arranging and superimposing them to create a finished work in which the art was in the judiciousness of their combination.

Apart from the handsome hand-finished petrol tank which proclaimed the identity of every BS, right from the primordial prototypical venture of 1919, very little was actually made in the little Brufsup works in Nottingham. The place was an assembly shop: engines came from J.A. Prestwich, and at other times from Barr & Stroud, MAG (Motosacoche à Genève), Matchless and even Austin; gearboxes from Sturmey Archer, forks from Montgomery, seats from Lycett, carburettors from anybody the customer fancied, and all the other miscellaneous bits and pieces from the industrial equivalent of Woolworths. It does not sound like a recipe for excellence or exclusiveness, but in fact GB set his component suppliers very high standards which they soon learned were worth meeting, such was the prestige that became associated with the BS. As for the exclusiveness, there were two sides to it: what could be more exclusive than a high-grade motorcycle, bespoke-tailored to the individual requirements of the customer, as early machines (and even the occasional later examples) often were? And what other manufacturer, with the possible exception of Alfred Scott, was so single-minded about making the sort of motorcycles that he personally liked, for the sort of riding that he personally did, and over the impressively wide range of speeds that he personally explored?

It was as much by his personal prowess on two wheels, in races and trials and sprints and record-breaking, as by his audacious marketing methods, that GB built that unquenchable reputation. In particular, after a brief but spectacular spell racing around the banked Brooklands circuit (where he was rumoured to have lapped at 100 mph, and to have established a record for distance covered while sliding on his backside after a tyre failure) he created a sprint special that had a fantastic run of successes. Sprints in those days were not the blasting matches that we see conducted on expansive airfield runways today: the venue was more likely to be the cambered pebble-dash drive from the gates of some private estate, a narrow and possibly tree-lined road on which BS terminal velocities of 100 mph or more must have been quite frightening.

The bicycle he created for this caper was a light, low, spindly affair that needed lateral trusses to stop it flexing in the middle when the taps were opened; and the engine was very special indeed, a 1000 cc sidevalve v-twin from the JAP development department, further tuned and tweaked by GB until it was probably the most powerful sidevalver that would ever be seen in a motorcycle for the next forty years. This was in 1922, and if a nickname had to be found for the bike, the public's memories of Bruce Bairnsfather's wartime cartoons guaranteed an affection for 'Old Bill'.

A nickname had to be found because GB knew that it helped publicity enormously. His original racer, always immaculate in its show finish, had been dubbed 'Spit-and-Polish', and it never went short of mentions in the motorcycling press. GB was a gifted publicist, an absolute master of public relations throughout his long career, with an eye for detail and an eye for the main chance that remained as acute as ever until his death in 1970. Indeed his rivals insist that all the aura of the Brough Superior was created not by good engineering but simply by good publicity. Probably GB's greatest aptitude was in pulling the wool over people's eyes; but he was a good rider, and his motorcycles did go fast. 'Old Bill' went so well that it recorded fastest time of day on 51 successive occasions when he sprinted it in 1922 and 1923; and in a sense it recorded FTD on the 52nd occasion – but alone, because a front tyre had failed again and GB followed the bike at ground level.

It was a fantastic run of successes. The big Brough Superior cracked records as a Nasmyth hammer cracks walnuts – and the analogy is not so farfetched, bearing in mind that practically all the opposition that GB's 1000 cc machine encountered was of 500 cc or less. Before long GB was not the only one asserting Brough superiority: Bert LeVack, Joe Wright, Alan Bruce, Arthur Simcock, Eric Fernihough, E.C.E. Baragwanath, and Noel Pope, all joined the heavy brigade, dragooning people inside and outside motorcycling into an uncritical adulatory acceptance of the rule of the Brough Superior.

The regal line that 'Old Bill' sired could be identified as the SS80, GB's best seller with a run of 624 specimens carrying the sidevalve 986 cc JAP engine from 1923 to 1932, and another 460 with a Matchless engine up to 1939. This was the machine that was to earn the tag of 'The Rolls-Royce of Motorcycles', perhaps the most notorious advertising slogan in the whole of motorcycling history. It was coined in a road test of the SS80 published in the magazine *The Motor Cycle*, and GB fell upon it with all the glee of an opportunist about to deprive someone of an even break. Whenever the slogan appeared – as it did with sickening frequency in his always extrovert and often extravagant advertising – GB was careful to attribute it to its source rather than appear to be making the claim himself. Nevertheless Rolls-Royce were concerned at this infringement of their copyright and presumed slight upon their inimitability: they despatched an emissary from Derby, upon whose arrival at Nottingham GB rose to the occasion as skilfully as always. The visitor was led into a section of the works where two white-coated men wearing white gloves were fussing over the fit and finish of the petrol tank on a machine that stood resplendent as few others before or since. The Rolls-Royce man was impressed and declared himself satisfied that the Brough Superior was manufactured to standards such as the Derby firm themselves observed: GB forebore to observe that the men were top-grade fitters preparing an exhibition machine for the forthcoming show at Olympia!

He always took the shows seriously, always planned to exhibit something that could be guaranteed to attract all the limelight. That was the explanation of the numerous one-off specials and short-run curios that he produced, typical oddities such as the transverse v-engined machines or the fatuous sidecar lugger with an Austin 7 engine and gearbox driving twin rear wheels, all of them doomed before they were ever made.

Yet there was one regular scene-stealer that was always meant to be taken seriously, and always had to be. If the SS80 had been regal, the SS100 was imperial. GB had been aware that the SS80 might be copied, just as he was always aware of the need to stay ahead of the pack. When Bert – strictly Herbert – LeVack put together a JAP-engined bolide with which to snatch the world speed record in 1924, GB saw that whatever the engine, and whatever the provenance of the rest of the machine (the front forks, of the bottom-link type, were from Harley Davidson), it had better appear in the record books as a Brough Superior, and had better display the appropriate petrol tank. On the *Route Nationale* near Arpajon, LeVack secured the record at 119.05 mph, furnishing GB not only with precious publicity but also with even more precious inspiration.

The outcome was a roadgoing BS that could exceed 100 mph, a bicycle so tried and tested that it would steer 'hands off' at that speed. At a time when the dreaded speed-wobble might affect an ordinary motorcycle at half as many miles per hour, this imperturbable stability counted for a lot and was demonstrated as often as GB judged necessary: the job usually fell to the lot of young Ron Storey, the works tester whose formidable exploits made him a legend in his own lifetime.

This lithe and architecturally graceful superbike, which came on the market in 1925, was the SS100; and whatever the letters stood for – Super Stable, Supra Sports, or Superior Steering – there was no mistaking the 100 part. Its prestige carried it through a run of 281 machines with JAP engines in the first ten years; and then, when Prestwich failed to toe GB's sternly drawn line, it continued with another 102 Matchless-engined specimens. Long before that stage was reached, it had sired the Pendine racer, the Alpine Grand Sports model that GB himself had ridden to victory in the Alpine Trial, and a number of record-breaking specials which reached as high as 169.5 mph when Eric Fernihough took a brief hold of the world speed record in 1937. The real romance of the SS100 was however with the road: it was the supreme mile-gobbler for the rider who demanded the best and could afford to pay for it. The price was always £170, which was a lot of money in those days; but as GB's blurb said, 'When considering the price of the Brough Superior, remember that the maker never intended to produce his design as cheaply as possible. It is a machine made to cater for the connoisseur rider who will have the best and fastest machine on the road.' It was bought by rich men and their sons, by princes and potentates, by sturdy individuals who believed in travelling fastest by travelling alone. Their standards were high: they demanded good performance, good looks, lasting reliability and a high standard of finish, and the BS was the obvious choice for the discriminating rider of the twenties with enough money to indulge his tastes. If he wanted to show off to everybody else he could have his SS100 silver plated, as did one of the Indian nobility; if he wanted to prove something to himself, he could wear out a rear tyre in a thousand miles between Saturday afternoon and Monday morning, as did Lawrence of Arabia;

George Brough himself with Joe Wright
astride a JAP-engined version of the
SS100, looking very much like the
Pendine racer. Note the tummy-pad and
regulation silencers for Brooklands
track.

ABOVE 'To what base uses . . . ?' If the BS was really so good, perhaps the SS100 version should be expected to do anything.

RIGHT Colonel T. E. Lawrence, alias Lawrence of Arabia, alias Shaw, alias (here) Aircraftman Ross, second son of Lord Chapman, scholar, archaeologist, soldier, spy, writer and rider of Boanerges which was one of the sons of thunder: 'A skittish motor-bike with a touch of blood in it is better than all the riding animals on earth.'

and if he wanted to complain, GB was always ready to listen.

Likewise GB was always ready to adopt new ideas to improve the SS100, whether they came from his own brain, his acolytes', or his opposition's. The front forks that came from Harley Davidson were redesigned in detail and patented as 'Castle' forks. There were ingenious prop-stands that folded out from beneath each footrest, brake adjustments that could be done with the fingers, headlamps that dipped, fly-screens, interconnected silencers to balance the beats from the unequal exhaust pipes, all sorts of detailed refinements to ease the lot of the hard rider.

Of course the whole thing was just an assembly of bits and pieces mostly bought out. Basically it was just a fully-looped cradle frame amply stayed to keep the rear wheel from straying, with a wicked-looking big pushrod v-twin engine to make it go, and not much in the way of brakes to make it stop. It was long and low and lean, and very nicely finished by the standards of its time, and as time went on it was regularly updated. Some of the revisions were impressive, such as the sprung heel which appeared in the late 1930s; but in general the changes betrayed the fact that GB himself was maturing. The SS100 grew heavier, perhaps more sluggish, and ceased to be the fastest thing on the road. GB himself was directing his attentions to quite another kind of motorcycle, one that might in fact deserve some of the accolades that his leaping vintage and neo-vintage thumpers never really merited, a smooth, refined, shaft-driven four-cylinder motorcycle that had long been his dream. At last he made it, and he called it the Golden Dream, and even if it did not work very well it was conceptually brilliant. It could have been developed, but the war brought other kinds of work to the BS factory, making (of all things) Merlin aero-engine crankshafts for Rolls-Royce. After the war the Dream was revived, but sadly rejected because it would have cost too much to make, too much by GB's reckoning for any likely customer to pay. Instead we were left with the memory of the SS100, the assembly job that in fact had at least one thing in common with the old Rolls-Royce, its susceptibility to the jibe that it represented the triumph of workmanship over design. In no other respect could it justly be called the Rolls-Royce of motorcycles, for George Brough was by no means as clever an engineer as he was cracked up to be; but his flair for publicity was exceptional, his salesmanship masterly, his involvement with real motor-cycling beyond question – and an adoring public wanted passionately to believe that the myth was true.

ABOVE RIGHT GB's Golden Dream, 1938.

Squariel as chariel – a four-piper in the
USA.

Ariel Square Four

When you have fully described the engine of the Ariel Square Four, you have said all that is worth saying about the entire motorcycle. This is not a condemnation of the 'Squariel', as it became known, for throughout its long career – it lasted 29 years, though the war accounted for a few of them – the majority of other motorcycles were no better in their frames and bicycle parts, and commonly lacked the distinction of so appealing an engine. Rather does all this amount to an illustration of the mentality of the people who bought motorcycles when the Square Four was designed, and while it remained current. They were interested enough in the power units, demanding in particular smooth running, quick response, and ample torque over a wide speed range; but they were uncritical of frame design, seldom taking their scrutiny much further than an examination of the quality of the enamelling. Riders in the luxury class were quite sure in their own minds about the engine characteristics they demanded, however, and in the Ariel Square Four many found full satisfaction.

Four-cylinder engines had been common for a quarter of a century when, in 1929, the Square Four was patented and put into production. Most of them had been designed with their cylinders ranged in-line, achieving satisfactory primary balance, but suffering the secondary vibrations consequent upon the disparity of connecting-rod angular accelerations on upward and downward strokes of the pistons. The narrow-angle v-four had been shown to be desirably compact and economical of material; and the horizontally-opposed four had at least been contemplated, although convincing examples of it were yet to be seen. By contrast the Ariel engine was bulky, heavy, and difficult to cool well enough to permit tuning to high specific performance factors; but it was incomparably smooth, satisfyingly quiet, and inordinately flexible – and enduringly popular for all these reasons.

It was designed by Edward Turner, who later achieved fame and distinction as designer of the vertical-twin Triumph motorcycle engine, and of V8 car engines for Daimler. The original patents were in his name, coupled with that of a member of the Sangster family with whom the history of the Ariel Company was for so long associated. In many of its best features and certainly its proportions the engine was typical of Turner, but for every patent boon there was a latent bane. Early examples had an overhead camshaft to operate the valves, but expense and noise eventually prompted a change to pushrods and rockers. Again, the earlier engines were lubricated by a primordial dip-and-splash method, each big-end plunging once per revolution into a trough of oil offered up beneath it, and replenished by a feeble little gear-pump in the sump. Porting was severely restricted, valves were perforce small and vertical, cooling air was with difficulty ducted to the rearmost cylinders, and satisfactory manifolding was difficult to achieve. Despite all this the Square Four was a great and continued commercial success, making it mildly surprising that no other manufacturer sought to copy it.

The arrangement of the engine entrained several virtues. The four cylinders

TOP The properties that made the Ariel single successful in scrambling and trials also encouraged sales to the army; but nasty high-speed steering discouraged the police from taking the Square Four.

ABOVE Another late four-piper, with ear-scratcher handlebars. Note the unusual Ariel link-and-plunger spring heel, intended to ensure constant chain tension.

Late Squariels betrayed the hand of the stylist, with echoes of Vauxhall flutes on the tank.

Never an outstanding performer in the
conventional sense, the Square Four was
always a favourite among long-distance
riders.

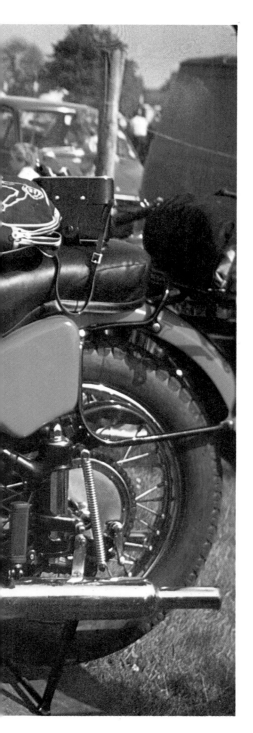

were arranged vertically and equidistant to form a square, the front two driving one crankshaft and the rear two being connected to another. These crankshafts were quite simple, and featured overhung crankpins upon which the roller-bearing big-ends were simply located; and between the circular crankwebs (or rather between the pair of main bearings inboard thereof) was a substantial flywheel in the form of a helically-toothed gear. The two flywheel gears meshed together, the arrangement being such that the crankpins of one shaft were at top and bottom dead centres while those of the other were at half-stroke. Thus balancing was virtually perfect, and the engine ran at all speeds from tickover to a quite healthy maximum rate with an absence of vibration or tremor that may still be considered exemplary.

Because of the relatively moderate flywheel mass and the multiplicity of cylinders, throttle response was pretty well immediate at all times, and this gave a feeling of real power as well as making possible gearchanges that were at once rapid and easy – for the torque characteristics of the engine encouraged close spacing of the ratios in the gearbox. Squariel riders liked to pretend that the effect was as though there were a direct connection between throttle twist-grip and speedometer needle, but it was not until the early 500 and 600 cc engines gave way to the modernized pushrod 1000 cc version that this illusion became easily tenable. In its full 1-litre form the Square Four could not only outstrip the majority of other vehicles it met on the road, it was also the peer of any in docility. The maximum speed of the big Square Four was reliably in excess of 90 mph, and sometimes three-figure speeds could legitimately be claimed; but at the other extreme it could shuffle along quietly at little more than walking pace and in top gear, pulling away with utter smoothness if the throttle were then opened.

This was what people wanted in the 1930s, especially those people who drove sidecar outfits. Only at the end of the decade was there beginning to be a demand for greater refinement of frame and bicycle components, which led to Ariel's introduction of a swinging-link form of rear suspension that was as unique as their engine. In later years the machine was to acquire quite good brakes, and eventually to be redesigned with cylinder blocks and heads of light alloy with individual exhaust header pipes to each cylinder, and with a general appearance sufficiently clean and neat to be as typical of its time as the gawky litter-strewn frame of the 500 and 600 was typical of the 1930s. But on a straight and well-surfaced road no rider of a Square Four would worry about these things, nor even be aware of them. His especial delight was in observing the rapport between twistgrip and speedometer needle.

Triumph Speed Twin

To have been everywhere, to have done everything, and to have sired an unaccountable number of illustrious bastards, must be qualifications for being considered, to put it mildly, accomplished. It follows that the Triumph Twin, in all its multifarious but so clearly related forms, must be considered a most accomplished motorcycle, for its record amounts to no less than that. Consider the Triumph Bonneville, the twin-carburettor derivative of the 650 cc Tiger 110 that set an American class record of 147.32 mph on the eponymous salt flats in Utah in 1958: it has at some time or other won every race for which it could feasibly be entered; it was for several years the fastest standard roadgoing motorcycle in production; it has taken, and on occasions held for long periods, sprint records in abundance. Its engine has powered machines that have captured the world speed record for two-wheelers, it has powered hill-climb cars, Formula IV racing cars, and sprint three-wheelers; and it became the special-builder's favourite engine for installation in a Norton frame so as to produce the enthusiasts' quondam dream machine, the Triton. Then there was its 500 cc relative the Daytona, developed by the sorcery of the same Doug Hele who so successfully cultivated the Bonneville, and on which the 1967 Daytona 200-miles race was won with miles in hand ahead of the once almighty Harley Davidson 750. It too was clearly bred from the original 500 cc Triumph Speed Twin, a 1938 trendsetter that was one of the most influential motorcycles in history.

Carefully styled so as to look in elevation like one of the popular two-port single-cylinder machines of the day, the Speed Twin's only particular feature for debate among the ultra-conservative British motorcycling public was that it had two cylinders. 'Two are better than one', as Ecclesiastes had told us ages earlier – and indeed there had been parallel-twin Triumphs in 1932 and even as early as 1912, though neither stayed the commercial course. Perhaps the difference about the Speed Twin was that it was designed by Edward Turner, who had come to Triumph after designing the Square Four for Ariel, and who was recognized as an engineer with great commercial insight. It was this sense that persuaded him that the smoother torque delivery, individually smaller reciprocating masses, more melodious exhaust, and better low-speed manners of the two-cylinder engine would endear it to the public when the workaday single-cylinder engine was suffered with as much familiarity and fatalism as one might accord a wart. Such engineering principles as Turner espoused were firmly repressed when they indicated that a 360° parallel four-stroke twin with equal firing intervals would, from the balance and vibration point of view, be as bad as two singles going *bump* together. To the customers this was of no account: they were more impressed by the smoothness resulting from the greater frequency of firing, contributing to an apparent overall improvement in smoothness of running. There was nothing else to distract them, for the new engine

BELOW Two 500 Triumphs, a 1909 belt-drive single and the 1948 Speed Twin.

fitted neatly into otherwise familiar surroundings, complete with the same gearbox and hubs and forks as they remembered in the single-cylinder Triumph Tiger 90. Apart from the smoother running, and the livelier performance, the difference was a matter of five pounds more or less – the Speed Twin was five pounds sterling dearer and five pounds avoirdupois lighter than the Tiger 90.

The performance seemed scintillating: at 6000 rpm the engine yielded 26 bhp, and a rider who knew how to tuck himself away could reach 90 mph. If he wanted more he could have it in 1939, when another five pounds would buy him the £80 Tiger 100, its engine polished internally and running a higher compression ratio. Yet another fiver would buy the optional aluminium-bronze cylinder-head. Yet another year, and the exigencies of war prodded Triumph into producing a generator unit with a light-alloy cylinder block and head of handsomely rectilinear proportions. In 1948 this superstructure was offered the underpinnings of a Tiger 100 to create the 500 cc Grand Prix racer, the prototype of which had won the Senior Manx GP in foul weather a couple of years earlier. It was not to enjoy much success thereafter, tending to shake itself to pieces in long events, though with restricted breathing the engine enjoyed enormous acclaim in the TR5 Trophy, which ran away with the International Six Days Trial of 1948 and was to be successful in all manner of rough-riding competitions for years afterwards.

When it came to racing, one of the most basic troubles with the Speed Twin and its immediate descendants was its bad handling and atrocious steering. The pre-war frame and forks were nothing to write home about; the early post-war ones were such as to justify strongly worded letters of complaint. The new telescopic forks were abysmally lacking in beam stiffness, given to binding and lozenging in all available planes, so easily distorted that the bicycle could be given a permanent limp by twitching the handle-bars while the front wheel was jammed between one's knees. At the rear, the ideal of minimal unsprung weight was pursued with a sprung hub that recalls Edmund Burke's warning that 'A thing may look specious in theory and yet be ruinous in practice.' The inspiration for this device is alleged to have been an ancient traction engine – scant excuse for the parts being so proportioned as to wear out rapidly, whereupon the wheel flipped about in a decidedly floppy manner, further to the prejudice of good order and navigational discipline.

In due course the sprung hub was to be replaced by the pivoted rear fork of the Tiger 110; but before this machine appeared, its predecessor had a very good run. This was the Thunderbird, which stayed in production from 1950 to 1966. The first three examples off the line averaged 90 mph for 500 miles around the bumpy concrete saucer of Montlhèry, finishing with a lap at over 100 mph. A good run of another sort was staged when the Thunderbird acquired an SU carburettor: this time the publicists dictated a 30 mph average around a 10-mile road circuit, in the course of which the Thunderbird averaged 155 mpg.

If speed was not as much of the T-bird's essence as it had been in the original 500 cc Twin, there was enough available to make it a very effective touring machine, forming the basis of a police mount that seemed destined to remain on duty for ever. Its steering and handling were scarcely of such quality as to

PREVIOUS PAGES
One of the Speed Twin's most favoured progeny was the 650 Bonneville, on which John Blanchard rides round the outside of a BSA in a 'production' race.
INSET The Speed Twin usually carried an exhaust pipe and silencer on each side, but this 1948 Triumph has been altered.

endear it to any policeman whose obligations forced him to ride fast, but it was nice and tractable at the low speeds which predominate in police work; and the low-compression single-carburettor Saint, the police special derived from later sporting 650s, enjoyed a charmed life at the hands of those who did the constabulary's buying. As for the riders who rode fast from choice rather than necessity, their prayers were answered when Doug Hele joined Triumph after the BSA amalgamation/takeover; it was he who improved the steering, filled out the power curve, and made the big twins and the little ones worthy of the reputation they had so long unjustly enjoyed.

The bitter truth about the Triumph Twin was that it was basically a bad motorcycle, despite which its engine was the one that persuaded a multitude that two cylinders were better than one, even though they both shook as one. It was copied by nearly everybody; and although most of the copyists made their own emendations, all they were left with in the end were engines that shared the inherent vices of Turner's Triumph. The Speed Twin had set the fashion, and the fiercely conservative British industry insisted that to depart from it would be folly. In the short term they were right, and they were confident that the long term would look after itself. The end was implicit in the beginning: the vertical twin made a fortune for the British industry, and set it on its rut-bound way to eventual disaster. 'A state without the means of some change is without the means of its conservation' – Edmund Burke again – and when the customers after some 30 years finally reached the limit at which fidelity and forbearance ceased to be virtues, the British industry was abandoned in a sorry state indeed. Perhaps good balance is a virtue that better merits cultivation.

Bonneville proper: on the salt flats of Utah, Bill Johnson sets a new 224.569 mph record with an unblown 80 bhp 650 Triumph engine in a bicycle that owes virtually nothing else to Triumph but a lot to Neracar and NSU.

Malcolm Uphill winning the 750 cm³ class of the 1969 Production TT on a T120 Bonneville.

Norton Manx

BELOW First, first time: Alec Bennett after winning the 1927 Senior TT on the first of the overhead camshaft Nortons.

OPPOSITE People believed it. There were times when it was true of the Manx racer, but it was not until the late 1950s that there was much that the production Norton and the racer had in common.

The apotheosis of the vintage motorcycle is represented by a model which first saw the light of day in 1927 and, in a derived form that was still clearly related, was still being raced seriously, if not successfully, in international events forty years later. 'Time will run back and fetch the age of gold' when the overhead-camshaft Norton reigned supreme in the Senior and – as often as not – the Junior categories in racing of the highest class from 1930 until, at the end of that decade, supercharged Europeans began to assert themselves. It was perhaps fortunate for Norton that when racing was resumed after the war the supercharger was proscribed; for the British machines by now seemed somewhat primitive, and had to be ridden hard to compete with Italians of similar or greater power and supposedly more refinement. Then there began an era in 1950 which lasted five years and must surely go down in history as the noblest in the Norton saga, when the classic single always fought the good fight, though by no means always did it win.

By this time the engine could no longer rival the power output of rivals boasting far more piston area, more revolutions per minute, more gearbox ratios, more forceful development and team organization. But, as Milton wrote in *Paradise Lost*, 'Who overcomes by force has overcome but half his foe': and what the Norton lacked in sheer power and consequent speed it made up for in a new roadworthiness that made its 'featherbed' frame the envy of all rivals, and gave the Norton handling qualities that made it the standard by which all others would be judged.

The UNAPPROACHABLE

Norton

The World's Best Road-Holder

Privateer T. McEwen on an over-the-counter Manx Norton being caught by works rider Geoffrey Duke winning the 1951 Senior TT.

With all that perversity for which motorcyclists in general and British motorcyclists in particular are notorious, people continued to identify the Norton by its engine. There must be an unwritten edict that 'by their engines ye shall know them', for other machines have been (perhaps) distinguished in the same way: for example the *Porcupine* AJS (long after it lost its quills), the *flat twin* Douglas (it could have been anything from a Great War army hack to a 90 Plus) or the *Cammy* Velo (which could be presumed the same thing whether the engine were to be found in a frame of the primordial flying-bedstead variety or the later air-sprung or lilo pattern). As with the Velocette, so with the Norton, it was its overhead camshaft that invested it with glamour, and to trace its glorious history we have to go back to the rudimentary squalor of 1927, to the days of reversed control levers, three-speed gearboxes with no positive stops in the selector mechanism, and frames that were designed with hacksaw and blowtorch.

In that year Walter Moore produced his first overhead-camshaft design, with which Norton scooped the Senior TT in the Isle of Man: the cylinder had a 79 mm bore, the piston a 100 mm stroke, and surmounting this 490 cm^3 monument to an already old tradition was something much more modern in the way of an aluminium box containing a single camshaft and adjustable rockers to convey its direction to the inclined overhead valves. It was a famous victory, at a good speed; and it had to satisfy Norton until 1931, by which time the engine design had been revised by Arthur Carroll. Minor changes were also made to the frame and bicycle parts, but they were insignificant compared with the revolution wrought in 1936 when the kidney-punching rigid frame was replaced by a sprung frame, improving the Norton's steering and roadholding (already good by the standards of its time) and giving the pilot a far more comfortable ride.

Thus enabled to keep both the wheels on the ground for a greater proportion of the time, the Norton riders could now exploit more power, and in 1937 they got it with a new engine enjoying twin overhead camshafts. By this time the capacity was 499 cm^3, and the following year the bore and stroke were revised again to 82 and 94.3 mm in the course of a redesign that enabled the engine to develop no less than 52 bhp at 6500 rpm, burning a mixture of petrol and benzol. This engine constitutes a landmark in the history of the unsupercharged petrol engine, the first (discounting a 1935 claim by Guzzi for their V-twin *Gambalunga*) to attain a specific performance factor exceeding 100 bhp per litre. It was development of inlet and exhaust pipes that did it, the exhaust in particular profiting from the use of a large megaphone which improved its resonating capabilities and made the most unholy din –

Two months later Duke won the Ulster GP and became the 500 cm^3 world champion.

> A shout that tore Hell's concave, and beyond
> Frightened the reign of Chaos and old Night.

After that, with the fuel regulations of post-war racing confining them to petrol, the Nortons never grew appreciably more powerful. They became a lot more reliable, as the interplay of metallurgy and mechanics made subtle changes to their shape and substance. Then in 1950 for a moment the engine was forgotten in the ecstatic contemplation of the new 'featherbed' frame. This had been designed by Rex McCandless of Belfast, and its virtues have variously been acclaimed as consummate or dismissed as contemptible by men who are

57

In 1952 at Codogno, Italy, the featherbed Manx with Duke aboard still had the legs of Gilera and Guzzi opposition.

learned and competent to judge and must therefore be right. It had four especial features, three of them being to its credit; and the fourth, being that it was composed of bent tubes and could therefore be neither as rigid nor as light as might be possible otherwise, was an accusation that could on different evidence be prosecuted with at least equal rigour against all its contemporaries. On the other hand the quite considerable width of the frame provided a desirably wide base from which to pivot the trailing fork which now carried the rear wheel; and it also enabled the engine to be located well forward, with beneficial effect upon the weight distribution of the machine as a whole and the sprung mass in particular. Finally, the crossing over of the frame tubes behind the steering head, so that the down-tubes were anchored to its top and the tank rails to its bottom, located the steering head in a manner much more free from stress and strain, from bending loads and distortion if you will, than had hitherto been accepted practice; and this must have been a vital contribution to the superb steering for which Norton's telescopic front forks usually received most of the credit.

In that year the Norton team enjoyed one other great advantage, the appointment to the spearhead of its riders of the newly emerged star Geoffrey Duke, whose racing career had begun only two years earlier. The style and skill of this impeccable rider complemented the roadholding of the new Norton perfectly, and the combination was virtually unbeatable for the next two years save when misfortune conspired to handicap him with bad luck or bad management. It was by exploiting the roadworthiness of this supremely dirigible motorcycle that the equally supreme Duke was able to bring to Britain laurels that, in view of the sheer power, speed and acceleration of rivals (notably the Gileras), should have gone to Italy. Only when at last he felt that he could stick his neck out no further did Duke transfer his allegiance to the Italian team; and thereafter it seemed that only luck kept the Nortons going as well as they did.

However, luck is a performance factor that defies calculation and mocks prognosis. After experimenting in 1955 with a redesigned single featuring an external flywheel and five-speed gearbox – and, for that matter, after toying with an ultra-low version whose cylinder lay horizontal like that of a Guzzi, with a four-cylinder engine built in the image of the Gilera, and with a balance sheet embarrassingly tinged with the traditional racing colour of Italy – they withdrew from official participation in classic racing.

They did not however abstain from the manufacture of racing motorcycles. Privateers could still buy and operate the now conventional 1954 pattern of Manx featherbed Norton with every expectation of reasonable competitiveness and ample enjoyment. Riders of such distinction as Hailwood and Minter confirmed their reputations while thus mounted, and many another demonstrated his prowess on it, riding at speeds which with the aid of streamlining and modern tyres allowed the Norton to remain in contention for an amazingly long time. With no other significant aids, Nortons increased their representative lap speeds by 8% between 1950 and 1960, during which period race-winning speeds based on the same representative events rose by 11%. Since then the Senior class has been in and out of the doldrums, and on occasions in the sixties when the mighty foreign manufacturers did not deign to participate, a Norton still sometimes won an important event. Its race of glory run and race of shame, and yet it could not be with them that rest: could even a Milton do it justice?

The apotheosis of the vintage motorcycle.

Gilera 500 four

If the featherbed Manx Norton of the 1950s can be called the finest vintage motorcycle of all time, the four-cylinder Gilera may be accounted the first and one of the finest of the moderns which supplanted it. It started as the Rondine, and started something that could never be stopped: the progress of motorcycling from the old bangers to the smooth modern street machines that are all related in principle to this once invincible and everlastingly glorious racer.

The Rondine was the product of a car manufacturer, CNA of Rome, who built in 1935 an out-and-out racing motorcycle whose design was extremely advanced for its time. It would have been enough that it was by the standards of its time so beautiful, but that would not have been surprising: it has always been a characteristic of Italian manufacturers that their designs should have about them that air of timeless rightness and formal beauty that are the inheritance of five centuries of pre-eminence in artistry and craftsmanship. However, the Rondine was amazing in its engineering too: the engine with four cylinders set in line across the frame, all sloping forward at 45° from the horizontal, was surmounted by two overhead camshafts driven from the centre of the crankshaft. Cooling was by water, the better to ensure the abstraction of heat from localized hot spots such as sparking plug bosses and exhaust ports – where temperatures would be expected to run very high because a Roots blower with triple-lobe rotors supercharged the engine to develop 60 bhp at 8500 rpm. The frame was by no means conventional, it and the forks being fabricated from steel pressings shaped to provide plenty of rigidity while yet embodying very little mass; and it was graced by a pivoting fork rear suspension, linked to unusual horizontal spring units. Yet another advanced feature was the saddle, elongated to permit a variety of riding positions in which the pilot could adjust himself to the demands of any given circuit. Today such a seat seems commonplace, but then the racing motorcycle usually had an absurd little saddle in the usual place for sitting up, and an absurd and even littler pillion on the rear mudguard for 'getting down to it' in the prone position for really high speeds.

However, if in 1935 the Rondine was setting fashions and winning a couple of races, it was setting no records and winning no emulation. In the following year a few examples were produced in roadgoing trim, and it seemed that the manufacturers were not taking their motorcycles seriously. Before long Gilera, who had already earned themselves a fine reputation in international trials with comparatively humdrum sidevalve motorcycles, took over the Rondine machine, which in due course reappeared with the original Giannini design not greatly altered (Rondine themselves had substituted a tubular frame for the pressed steel original late in 1935) despite its wearing the Gilera badge.

With the new name came a new aura of purpose, and people began to consider how serious might be the onslaught made by such a machine upon motorcycle racing. With so much complication in its design and so much nicety involved in its construction, the Gilera would inevitably be a very expensive machine; but the smooth torque delivery, the low transmission loadings, the high

OPPOSITE ABOVE When even Duke could not keep the Norton ahead of the Gilera, he started riding for Gilera, whose rider Umberto Masetti won the 1952 Senior Championship. For the next three years it was Duke's, on the refined and elegant four-cylinder machine of which this is a 1954 version.

OPPOSITE BELOW By 1957 fairings had developed encouragingly, and the Gilera four in its streamlined dustbin was supreme among racing motorcycles. Alas, full fairings were to be banned, and this fight between two Gilera streamliners at Monza in 1957 was to be one of their last appearances.

ABOVE Gilera team manager Piero Taruffi was also a former racing rider and a practising racing-car driver. All these and his engineering training came together when he set new standing-start records for the kilometre and the mile in the 500 cm³ car class with this Gilera-engined twin-boom car, the Tarf.

61

piston and valve areas, and the high rates of crankshaft rotation made possible by four short-stroke cylinders, all combined to produce a performance that at any rate in theory should be invincible. In fact the Gilera made little mark on racing in 1938, nor was much attempt made to do so; but it did demonstrate its performance, concerning which few had any doubts, and its reliability – upon the want of which many based their hopes of remaining competitive. It set a new world record for motorcycles at 170.37 mph and covered more than 121 miles in an hour. In 1939 the record-breaking Gilera, once again with the Italian doyen of engineer-racers Piero Taruffi tucked inside the streamlining, lifted the hour record to nearly 127 miles, by simply batting up and down a 28-mile length of autostrada and being humped around at each end because the turning circle was so unwieldy. In road racing form the machine was wieldy enough to win the European 500 cc Championship.

In 1946, with the war over, the Gilera four reappeared in the hands of Nello Pagani to win the Italian Championship of that year. It did not look much different from the pre-war machine, save that the supercharger had gone, for forced induction was proscribed by the new rules governing racing. The Porcupine AJS was to demonstrate the folly of attempting to develop in unblown form an engine conceived for supercharging, but Gilera were making no such mistake: there was promise of a completely revised racing four to appear in 1947, with air cooling, wet-sump lubrication (the original bike had displayed a very glamorous and profusely ribbed aluminium oil tank along its flanks), and cylinders that were a little less near the horizontal. Things were, alas, still difficult in Italy, where recovery from the ravages of war was a little slow, and it was not until 1948 that the new machine appeared. It was the work of engineer Remor, who was to leave Gilera at the end of 1949 and go to MV Agusta to start designing the same sort of machine all over again for them; and it was very much as forecast. There was still some similarity to many of the earlier frame components, such as the pressed steel blade-type front forks and double trailing-arm rear forks; and the effectiveness of the weight saving designed into the apparently massive double cradle frame was proved by the modest 257 lb weight of the complete machine.

Its racing debut in the Dutch TT was impressive but not overwhelming. For the next couple of years it was at its best only on the faster circuits, where its riders would often play along with the competing British Nortons, keeping pace with them while sitting up, and only getting down to it for the final couple of laps, to roar away from the single-cylinder machines with contemptuous ease. In 1951 the superior handling of the Manx Norton and the virtuosity of its rider Geoffrey Duke were more than a match for the power of the Italian machine on more twisting circuits, and it was he who took the championship. By 1952 even the Norton's outstanding roadholding and the peerless ability of Duke could not hold the Gileras at bay, even on the tighter circuits: by this time the frame design had been brought much more up-to-date, a tubular cradle frame of modern concept being matched to equally modern telescopic front forks and to a coil-sprung trailing rear fork, with proper hydraulic damping of both sets of suspension. Indeed the Italian machine earned its manufacturers the appropriate World Championship in 1952 and again in 1953, when the team was joined by Duke. He brought with him Avon tyres from England, and an impeccable riding technique which combined with the paralyzing performance of the Gilera to win the Grands Prix of Holland, France, Switzerland and the Nations, and another pair of world titles, one for the rider and one for the manufacturer.

In 1954 he did much the same again, winning even more races; and by now the machine winning the Constructors' Championship had a redesigned frame, suspension and brakes (twin-cam central drum types, with alternative drum sizes for the front wheel according to the demands of each circuit), and a five-speed gearbox. During that year it also acquired more extensive streamlining, the original vestigial front fork shroud eventually giving way at the GP des Nations to a complete 'dustbin' fairing enveloping the front wheel. No machine could better exploit the streamlining, for there was no other in racing to match the power of the Gilera, and there is nothing like aerodynamic drag for wasting power. By this time the elegant four-cylinder engine was developing 64 bhp at 10,500 rpm, an output more than 18% greater than that of the 500 cc single-cylinder Norton which so often sought to give it battle. Only the 60 bhp engine of the 500 cc flat-twin Rennsport BMW could approach the power of the Gilera, and the BMW was not in the same class when it came to handling, though it was a power to be reckoned with in sidecar events. Nevertheless the Gilera began to do well in sidecar events too, in the hands of riders such as Ernesto Merlo; and in any case the power output of the Gilera continued to rise until by 1957 it was more like 70 bhp. That was a wonderful year, in which the late Bob McIntyre established the first lap of the Isle of Man TT circuit at more than 100 mph in the course of winning the Senior event (lengthened to 302 miles that year) at the record speed of 98.99 mph. Later that year McIntyre set a new one-hour record of 141.37 miles around the bumpy banking of the track at Monza, and did it on the 350 cc Gilera.

At the end of 1957 the firm withdrew from racing, and although they attempted a modest comeback in the 1960s, it was a half-baked business that is best forgotten. Far better to remember the Gilera four in its heyday, as the fastest and most consistently successful racing machine in the Senior class, as the holder for a remarkably long term of the world record for a kilometre covered from a standing start on two wheels, and as the origin of one of the most soul-stirring noises ever to enrapture the ears of men.

Gilera built a 350 cm³ four in the style of the 500, and despite the Guzzi domination of the Junior class the Gilera was not without some successes. Here Libero Liberati rides it out sidesaddle to practice at Monza for the 1957 GP des Nations.

The Gilera 500 four in 1952 trim, before the days of Geoffrey Duke and Avon tyres. Gileras raced with large or small front brakes, according to the demands of the circuit.

Vincent
Black Shadow

'Follow a shadow, it still flies you; seem to fly, it will pursue.' So sang Ben Jonson to support his contention that women are but men's shadows; but his words rang truer more than 300 years later when the first Black Shadow rolled out of the Vincent HRD factory at Stevenage. For this was the world's fastest standard production motorcycle when it went into production in 1948, and it remained the fastest long after the Vincent firm had despairingly given up their idealistic business of building the best motorcycle they possibly could for that diminishing band of riders who could both appreciate it and pay for it. Well into the 1960s, wrapped in a mystique carefully cultivated by many fanatically enthusiastic owners, the big Vincent still had that commanding air about it when you met one on the road, and many a rider of avowedly super-sporting machinery was humiliated by having some much older Black Shadow come galloping past, its rider raked in that peculiar and distinctive riding position – feet wide apart, hands close together, the body leaning forward against the wind, slack as a sack of potatoes but as well poised as a prize-fighter. It was a machine about which legends could be and were made, but about which the truth would serve well enough.

Quite apart from its performance, which encompassed a maximum speed of about 125 mph in original standard tune on noisome 80 octane petrol, the truth about the big Vincent was quite simply that it was a masterpiece. It cost a lot of money, but even an examination of the detail work evident on its exterior showed that it was money well spent. For example, there was a full range of adjustment for the gear lever, the brake pedal, the footrests, the handle-bars and anything else that could conceivably require adjustment; tommy-bars allowed really rapid wheel removal, with no tools necessary but a pair of pliers for undoing the spring-clip on a chain-link if removing the rear wheel; the brakes and the chain tension could be adjusted by finger; and when for the Series C version the old Brampton front forks were replaced by Vincent's own Girdraulic, the trail and spring rate could be altered simultaneously for solo or sidecar work in a minute or two.

Yet these details hold much less than the full truth about the splendour of the Vincent's design. It was the progeny of a marriage between two fascinating minds, the creatively imaginative and idealistic Englishman Philip Vincent, and the ingenious and practical Australian Phil Irving. Perhaps the whole motorcycle was greater than the sum of its parts, but any one of those parts bore witness to the complementary interaction of those antipodean brains. The Girdraulic forks gave a clue: their geometry was similar to that of the traditional girder forks, their springing and damping media were such as were generally associated with the then increasingly popular telescopic forks, while the mechanical strength, and (more important) stiffness, were superior to either. Each fork blade was a high-duty alloy forging, and the whole structure was

ABOVE Decidedly non-standard aft of the gearbox, this Vincent 1000 Rapide reminds us that many riders thought the big twin one of the most promising 'development' vehicles in existence. The developments did not always constitute improvements.

OPPOSITE As intended: the Series C Black Shadow, world's fastest standard production motorcycle.

66

completely free from the sloppiness, binding, flexibility, and general trochaic irregularity that afflicted most other kinds of front suspensions.

It was indeed in its structure that the Vincent was most distinguished and least appreciated. If it be accepted as a prerequisite of good steering and handling in a motorcycle that its wheels be retained relative to each other and to the steering head in those planes they were intended by the designer to occupy, then it must be admitted that frame stiffness, all the way from wheel spindle to wheel spindle, is of extreme importance; and in this respect the Vincent had few, if any, rivals. Paradoxically it had little or no frame – just a sheet-steel box concealed by the fuel tank, extending from the steering head to the rear spring and damper unit, and having the engine slung beneath by the two cylinder heads. The rear fork or sub-frame was pivoted on taper roller bearings in an anchorage on the rear of the particularly massive crankcase and transmission casting, and the rigidity of the engine structure was so immense as to impart to the machine as a whole a beam, and more particularly a torsional, stiffness such as only the space-frame of the racing Guzzi of the mid-1950s could be presumed to equal. Only the rear fork sub-frame betrayed the design by being visibly imperfect in its stressing: it was only partially triangulated, and it seems that even Vincent could not avoid the contagion of curved tubes.

The engine repaid close study. Little could be gleaned *ab extra*, save that it was clearly intended to generate and dissipate some considerable heat, being enamelled black all over. It was also clear from the disposition of the pushrod tunnels that the camshafts were located deliberately high in order to minimize the valvegear's reciprocating mass, a technique that the machine inherited from pre-war HRD engines. Further ingenuity in the valve design placed the rockers half-way down the valve-stems, engaging a shoulder, while the valve springs were up at the thin end, as remote as possible from the sources of heat.

Yet it was the bottom half of the 55° v-twin Vincent engine that was most meritorious. Engine and gearbox were conceived as parts of the same structure, the massive light-alloy castings being stiffened by substantial internal walls to produce a construction in which all bearings were positively located, all loads were properly distributed, and all components were constrained to remain precisely where they were put. Every exposed face-joint was free from the imposition of such loads as might cause distortion and oil leaks. Materials were as good as could be obtained at the time, and where performance could be improved by surface polishing this was done, as in the case of connecting rods, rockers and ports.

This passion for proper distribution of mechanical loads was indulged not only in the engine and transmission but even in the brakes. Each wheel carried two of these, one on each side, so as to balance the stresses to which the wheel and forks were subjected. The brakes were not particularly big, amassing between them only 36 square inches of lining area, which admittedly was more than most machines of the day, but less than a few could boast. Nevertheless they were shown to work very well, and on many occasions the Vincent was proved capable of stopping at rates of deceleration considerably exceeding *g*. Apparently the ribbed cast-iron brake-drums of the Black Shadow, replacing the steel drums of the basically similar Rapide tourer, ensured reasonable retention of this braking ability, for the Black Shadow did quite well in contemporary racing despite its then considerable weight. Years later its weight seemed by no means excessive, for the BSA 500 of the late 1950s weighed only 20 lb less, the Triumph 3-cylinder 750 of the late 1960s weighed 30 lb more, and the 1000 cc Honda of the mid 1970s is heftier by a hundredweight.

Today also there are five or six roadgoing motorcycles in full production which can reach speeds higher than those that the Black Shadow established as within its compass. It is almost a measure of their extremity that they can do it, as it is a measure of the Vincent's that it did it all so much earlier. Nor do they all do it with that same ineffable ease of manner. An Earl, who could be expected to be authoritative on the subject, once defined the mark of the true aristocrat as 'effortless superiority': on this reckoning the Black Shadow can claim true nobility.

OVERLEAF
Quite apart from clever major features such as the Girdraulic front forks, the big Vincent was one of the most conscientiously detailed motorcycle designs ever seen.
INSET The Series D Vincents (this is a Rapide) had a fully sprung seat, a single rear brake, and the hand-levered stand which had been a feature of some Rudge machines in the late 1930s.

BELOW Different handlebars and brake drums, less black about the engine, more generous mudguarding and less flamboyant instruments, distinguished the Series C Rapide from the Black Shadow.

RAPIDE

VINCENT

The competition Douglas of the 1920s was fascinating and formidable, and this one of 1927 vintage reveals a design philosophy that had much in common with that of the 350s which came a generation later.

Douglas 90 Plus

Most of the motorcycles commended in this volume enjoyed in their time considerable success, if not universal acclaim; but the transverse-twin Douglas did not. Any reader more concerned with the design of history than with the history of design might therefore demand why it should be included. It is here because of what it was at a time when none of the others were – a refreshingly modern motorcycle. It is here also because of what it could have been, which is something most of the others never even aspired to – an influence for good, in a movement where all others were obsessed with the perpetuation of mediocrity. Why then did it fail, and what blighted its fortunes?

Eminent critics (the epithet is as necessary as sops were for Cerberus) have pronounced that the Douglas failed because it was a bad motorcycle. It was nothing of the sort. It was however bad business – which eminent men of commerce (the need for the epithet is more dubious) would have us believe is more important. Let the accountants tell their wretched tally, for we can cite many cases to show that reward does not wait upon virtue.

When the 90 Plus was first publicly shown late in 1949, Douglas were already in the hands of the Receiver; so it is impossible to deny that it was bad business. The ordinary touring and semi-sporting machines that the Bristol firm had introduced soon after the war were outstandingly modern in concept, and that was really the root of the trouble: it was a time when the public was adamant in its insistence that a motorcycle should continue to resemble the crude, uncultivated, springless and vibratory monuments to engineering cluelessness

Low build, long wheelbase, a properly balanced engine – a Douglas is a Douglas, whether 1913 or 1948. Astride the more modern transverse twin is F. J. Poppe, son of Douglas technical director Erling Poppe, who in 1948 had just joined the company after designing the unusual and beautiful Sunbeam twin.

that decades of reaction and parsimony had persuaded them were appropriate to their desires. To be fair, the Douglas resembled in superficial layout the ABC that Granville Bradshaw had produced more than 30 years earlier. It was also redolent of the shaft-drive transverse-twin Endeavour that Douglas had put on the market in 1935, and which they took off again after an unhappy couple of years in which only about fifty examples were sold. This simply makes it even more disgraceful that in 1950 the Douglas should still be too far ahead of its time.

With the exception of the chain drive to the rear wheel (shaft drive had been judged too costly) the specification of the post-war 350 was virtually a summary of all the boons that an open-minded and progressive rider might enjoy. The stiff double-loop cradle frame, the immensely stiff trailing rear forks with torsion-bar springing (and strangely no dampers, although friction in the connecting linkage probably helped), the bottom-link front forks – again immensely stiff – with torque-arms parallel to the suspension links so as to leave the springing unaffected by braking, the utterly smooth horizontally opposed engine, bore and stroke virtually equal at 60.8 and 60 mm respectively, all these things marked the Douglas as being outstanding in its freedom from the obsolescence that seemed deliberately built into the conventional motorcycle of its time.

Of course it was not perfect: the frame tubes used to fracture above the rear lug on early models and had to be strengthened for the 90 Plus; the enormous and generously cooled front brake was only as good as its 9 inches diameter suggested so long as all the linkages and bushes associated with it were in perfect condition; and the engine had a rather voracious appetite for big ends.

BELOW Heavily finned barrels and heads, an airscoop to cool the clutch, a polychromatic gold finish, and an evident need for copious crankcase ventilation, were features of the 90 Plus.

RIGHT As supplied in road trim, the 90 Plus had all the accoutrements (such as the cast aluminium toolbox panniers) of the touring 350 Douglas; but that 9-inch front brake, finned and ventilated, set in a large-diameter wheel and so linked to the outstandingly good front forks as to isolate the front suspension from brake torque interference, bore witness to super-sporting potential.

The other side of that Plus front brake shows more clearly the four-bar linkage upon which brake and suspension geometries were based. The lower link, a massive forging, transmitted wheel movements to a progressive-rate spring and two-way hydraulic damper within the very rigid fork stanchion.

The run-of-the-mill 'Mark' model of the 350 Douglas was basically as similar to the Plus model as the shaky state of the manufacturers might have led one to expect.

Nevertheless, the 90 Plus in its roadgoing form was the fastest 350 that might be encountered on the street in its day, the best braked, the most comfortable, and the most sure-footed in its handling. Exploiting its then respectable 25 bhp and its four most delightfully close ratios in a gearbox that displayed none of the shortcomings generally associated with engine-speed transmissions, allowed the 90 Plus to outperform the majority of 500 cc road machines among its contemporaries.

This was hardly sufficient to justify its existence, for the 90 Plus was conceived and marketed as a machine that could double in the role of a clubman's racer, either by being converted from roadgoing specification or by being bought in racing trim. However, to attract custom, it first had to show itself competitive, and in this it never really succeeded.

Having a Receiver about the house can be very inhibiting. A properly backed official racing programme could simply not be entertained; so the machine's designer Eddie Withers had to conduct the 90 Plus racing campaign as a largely private venture, assisted by the late F.W. Dixon and a shoestring or two. Lavish preparation of the racing machines was out of the question, as was the employment of star riders. The fact that the 90 Plus gave a fairly good account of itself, in events such as the Clubman's TT or the Hutchinson Hundred, despite these crippling deficiencies suggests that it was in fact a far better machine than the results sheets indicated.

In competition trim it usually mustered 27 bhp at 7500 rpm, but this did not suffice to make it fast enough for genuine racing company, in which its presence was best justified by its outstanding roadworthiness. Withers therefore set about the preparation of some special Dixon engines, in which by careful attention to crankcase breathing (to eliminate pumping losses), to bearings and lubrication, and in particular to cam design, he contrived to uprate the engine to 31 bhp at no less than 10,000 rpm, the engine remaining safe up to 11,000 – an astonishing figure for a pushrod machine. In this form the 90 Plus proved able to reach 108 mph on the Sulby Straight and to run up to its full 11,000 rpm in top gear, equivalent to 119 mph, down Bray Hill.

Despite these modifications and others, including twin-leading-shoe operation of the front brake, the 90 Plus never really achieved anything of consequence. Its best was a fourth place in the 1950 Clubman's TT. As a road machine, however, it remained one of the most sensually satisfying of all motorcycles, as delightful to ride as it was rewarding to contemplate. In road trim it really could exceed 90 mph as its name implied, while its splendid balance and navigational imperturbability must have saved many more necks than mine. None of these things seemed to be able to save the company, however, and production of the 90 Plus was discontinued in 1953 when 250 had been made, every one being issued with a dynamometer report guaranteeing at least 25 bhp. Engines that failed to reach this standard were coupled to wide-ratio gearboxes, fitted into a maroon bicycle called the 80 Plus, and sold for road use only. Before long Douglas gave up making motorcycles altogether, and concentrated on trying to make Vespa scooters and a profit. The dictum of Shakespeare, 'No profit grows where is no pleasure taken', would never convince an accountant.

Guzzi 350 bialbero

In their full frontal fairings, the particoloured racing motorcycles of the mid-1950s were a glamorous sight. The Gilera was dazzling in crimson and white, the MV Agusta splendid in scarlet and silver, the BMW immaculate in the purest glossiest white imaginable. When the Moto Guzzi team wheeled their racers on to the grid, they lowered the tone of proceedings considerably, trundling out a long low motorcycle that looked like nothing else in sight. It did not even have a traditionally handsome sculpted petrol-tank looming like a pediment above the rest of the structure: if you could have a close peep, the petrol-tank might be found slung beneath the top rails of a decidedly odd-looking chassis frame, a simple cylindrical metal tank steadied by a couple of pieces of wood. As for the wax-polished gloss of a lovingly burnished paint finish on the fairing, there was nothing of the sort, only a barely opaque blow-over of dull greenish undercoat. Yet this was the machine, this skimpy and scruffy contraption, that captured the world 350 cc championship in 1955, 1956, and 1957, defending it and a Moto Guzzi tradition against all the weight of multi-cylindered or brilliantly ridden opposition from rival factories.

The weight of the opposition was the clue. The reason for the Guzzi appearing in its cobweb-thin undercoat was that an extra layer of paint would burden it with unnecessary weight. It was the same reason that prompted engineer Carcano to stick to a single-cylinder engine, which must be lighter than a multi of similar displacement and engineering style, the same reason that prompted him to employ 10 mm sparking plugs instead of the more usual and less heat-sensitive 14 mm size, to eliminate the cast-iron liner in the cylinder by having the bore hard-chromed, to control the valves with single helical springs instead of the usual doubles or even triples, and the reason why the chassis was a trellis-like spaceframe instead of the usual ill-stressed agglomeration of bent beams and flying buttresses. Just as one should only travel by first class train when no Pullman is available, Carcano only used aluminium where magnesium was unsuitable, treating iron and steel as third class tickets to some very poverty-stricken engineering.

Giulio Carcano was a real engineer, not one of those jumped-up mechanics who used to be so abundant in the design offices of the established motorcycle manufacturers until their inability to rise to the challenge of the 1960s brought them to their knees. He recognized that the most important aspect of high-speed motorcycling was the overcoming of inertia, and that the smaller the mass that had to be given a change of velocity or direction, the more easily it could be done. That was why he waged his relentless campaign against weight, which he strove to keep low both figuratively and literally, so that his relatively low-powered racers could accelerate and corner and brake as well as any of their rivals. He also recognized the importance of aerodynamic drag since, while inertia increases in proportion to the mass, resistance to motion through the air increases as the square of the velocity. Here was another reason for keeping the motorcycle very low, to minimize frontal area, as well as for streamlining it to

The last and least developed of Ing. Carcano's racing marvels was the 500 cm³ V8 Guzzi. Dickie Dale relaxes on it after finishing fourth in the 1957 TT.

79

improve its coefficient of penetration: so, while other factories left the design of their racing fairings to draughtsmen or panel-bashers, Carcano saw to it that Moto Guzzi had their own full-scale wind tunnel.

Given a full-frontal fairing to cleave the air, there was no point in trying to create a slim-line traditional frame inside it. Instead Carcano logically exploited the opportunity to make a frame as light and as stiff in all directions as the space thus liberated would permit, integrating the resulting triangulated trellis of small-diameter tubes with the fairings so that the weight of the normal fairing-supporting struts was eliminated.

All this was new for 1955. The rest, though continually refined, was inherited. The original 350 single was the brainchild of that lanky but athletic and very shrewd rider Fergus Anderson, almost certainly the brainiest of the Guzzi team: he reckoned that the five-speed 250 Guzzi was so good (at the time it had just won its seventh TT and its third world championship in four years) that if the bore and stroke were increased it should have a fair chance of doing well in the 350 class in 1953. Carcano took him up on his suggestion, and in a first exploratory move enlarged the single-camshaft engine to 320 cc. This meant a drop in specific output, from 114 bhp per litre to 97; but it was enough to allow Anderson to carry off the German Grand Prix, and score a very respectable third place in the Junior TT. That was all the encouragement Carcano needed before building a full-sized engine, with a little more power and a usefully wide spread of torque. At the end of the season, Anderson had the title he had sought. In 1954 he won it again.

The much more advanced machine that Guzzi fielded in 1955 carried an engine that had been extensively redesigned. The cylinder head, fed by a carburettor of sousaphone-like proportions at the remote end of a remarkably long and nearly vertical induction pipe, was capped by two camshafts, carried two coil-sparked plugs, and developed 35 bhp, enough to take the championship yet again – and again in 1956. Despite the long induction tract, low-speed torque was not as good as it had been in earlier years, so Carcano embarked once again on revising the breathing and burning departments while still taking off weight at every opportunity. The result was an engine safe up to rpm as high as the 250 used to run (8400), and with such ample mid-range torque that gear ratio problems became a thing of the past. The high volumetric efficiency that was responsible for this torque remained evident at the peak of the power curve: where the old 250 had a peak-power bmep of 176 lb/in², and the subsequent 320 and 350s a more modest 166, the 1957 350 reached 181, pushing the maximum power up to 38 bhp. It was enough to do the trick yet again.

It was enough only because of the excellence of Carcano's engineering elsewhere in the motorcycle. Minimizing aerodynamic drag was important too, as was minimizing mass and the height of the centre of gravity, even if it meant having a pump to raise petrol from a low-slung tank to the relatively high carburettor. None of this can be fully effective unless the tyres are kept on the ground and pointing in the right directions: the suspension of the lightweight Guzzi was exceptionally good. This was despite, not because of, the lightness of the machine, since a fundamental of good suspension design is that the ratio

ABOVE Ken Kavanagh on the 1954 Guzzi 350.

RIGHT One associates the Guzzi single with streamlining in the 1950s, but this is ridiculous: Luigi Cavanna set fourteen new world records on an *Autobahn* in August 1952, riding this faired 250 Guzzi with sidecar.

This 1954 Guzzi, ridden by a jocular Fergus Anderson, has an enclosed rear wheel to reduce drag still further.

of sprung to unsprung masses should be high. Carcano got around this problem by rejecting conventional front forks, most of which are unsprung and mechanically sloppy: his preference was for fairly long and carefully angled leading links at the bottom of stiff fork-legs that were part of the bicycle's sprung mass, the hub describing such an arc on the end of the links as to ensure the maintenance of good steering geometry over an ample range of wheel deflection. Since it had less torque to resist than the corresponding item in other more powerful machines, the trailing rear fork presented no problems. Between these two extremities, set well apart by a wheelbase long enough to minimize the effect of pitching moments, was suspended a bicycle whose centre of gravity and centre of gyration were so placed as to keep the ride smooth, the control crisp and the wheel adhesion blameless whether the whole thing were being flicked from bank to bank, accelerated hard under the impulsion of all that torque, or braked even harder with the aid of drums that somehow always looked bigger than everybody else's. The whole thing weighed only 216 lb, could exceed 140 mph, and offered so little inertia and so little resistance to motion that its fuel consumption at racing speeds was no less than 35 miles per gallon.

It was at that point that Moto Guzzi retired from racing. The low-slung single, after generations of being one of the leading lightweights, and five years of being the champion junior, and promising to be one of the most valuable weapons in the senior or 500 cc armoury that Carcano completed with an in-line four-cylinder engine and a transverse water-cooled V8 (with the idea of using whichever one best suited a given circuit), was to be seen no more. It could never have been the same again, for the FIM tied their corporate mind into the most insolubly obscure knot and prohibited proper streamlining. Without that, and therefore without the clever frame, the Guzzi could never have been the same. It was one of the governing body's greatest blunders, arresting the development of motorcycle design and causing a stultification that remains apparent nearly twenty years later. They argued that they were doing it for safety's sake – but the only cause of full fairings tending to provoke directional instability in cross-winds (as on some bikes they did) was the utterly arbitrary dimensional limits imposed on those fairings by the FIM themselves many years earlier. The tragedy could perhaps have been averted, but that would have needed many more men in racing as clever as the regrettably unique Carcano.

Three Moto Guzzis, two Gileras, and one MV Agusta line up on the front row of the starting grid for the Belgian 350 cm³ Grand Prix of 1957. What a great year that was!

BMW R69S

There is something rather special about German engineering, something that manifests itself as much in motorcycles as in their other products. It is something that implies a meticulous attention to detail and to finish, an innate compulsion to be absolutely thorough in the engineering of even the meanest component in a large and sophisticated complex. This philosophy shows up well in the motorcycles produced by BMW: where lesser manufacturers might make odds and ends out of sheet pressings, BMW will use costly forgings or elaborate castings. Where others will fob off a cosmetically sensitive customer with a quick blow-over of metallic paint and some splashes of meretricious chromium, the BMW – at least until a few years ago – was dressed as expensively, soberly, and inconspicuously as any Brummell could desire.

The painstaking design and workmanship that produced such a convincing exterior (despite all those bent tubes) produced a correspondingly honest interior, with the result that the BMW was impressively durable. In the late 1950s, when most competing brands were finding their market collapsing, it was general practice to juggle for sales with the aid of trumpery tricks from the merchandising man's armoury of deceptions, rather than to commit scarce

BELOW Sober city black-and-stripes: the R69S was in fact the 42 bhp pride of the BMW line, capable of 110 mph without raising its voice. Note the adjustable rear springs, then novel, and the Earles front forks, now quaint.

OPPOSITE The competition history of the BMW motorcycle is almost as long as its technical history, and almost as continuous. The original R32 was raced as early as 1924, rider Franz Bieber becoming *Deutscher Strassenmeister* (there's an eloquent term!) in the 500 cm³ class.

money to the improvement of a product whose proprietor too often fondly supposed incapable of improvement. It was not so with BMW: they were finding times hard too, as an increasingly prosperous Germany acquired a taste for something bigger and better in *Prunkwagen* and spurned the motorcycle that had served it so well. Despite the introduction of a whole range of quiet, impeccably mannered, and beautifully finished luxury motorcycles of utterly distinctive specification and appearance in the 1950s, the end of the decade saw BMW's motorcycle sales topple from six and a half thousand a year to a beggarly four thousand, almost all overseas. Yet they kept their standards, refusing in any way to compromise whatever excellence they had attained.

Their customers might have been few, but they were discerning and faithful – and, being clearly men of appreciable means if they could afford one of these impressively expensive machines, influential. It was a curious situation but in the long term a rewarding one, for whilst those riders remained faithful to BMW, the factory in turn was to remain faithful to them: instead of doing what had been threatened and closing down their motorcycle plant, BMW were to celebrate the revival of interest in motorcycling late in the 1960s with the perfectly timed production of brand new models produced in a new motorcycle factory, and to have that faith in turn rewarded by a monumental increase in sales.

In many ways the latest BMW bahnstormers are essentially similar to all their predecessors. It may be unfortunate that, although they undoubtedly go better and probably are even more reliable than those that went before them, they look rather more brash – rather like somebody who, after generations spent in becoming a gentleman, suddenly discovers that it is much more fun being a rake. The accountants may not agree, for accountants have their own

peculiar views about such things, but historians may yet decide that the BMW motorcycles that really earned the firm its reputation were the R50/60/69S of that crucial period when the firm was struggling to remain both respectable and alive.

That was a time when the BMW had become the favourite mount, perhaps the only possible mount, of the really long-distance rider. There were the coast-to-coast escapaders of the USA, carving whole hunks off established two-wheel records between the Pacific and Atlantic; and there were servicemen who saw the BMW as a pleasant way of coming home to Britain on leave from the Far East and returning, perhaps two or three times in a tour of duty. The big black Bavarian just seemed to go on and on, never breaking things, never sweating oil, never issuing more than the most apologetic murmur of exhaust noise. They were perhaps the most civilized motorcycles in the world.

Curiously, they behaved as though BMW had thrown out the brio with the barbarity. There were, and have always been in the firm's history, BMW motorcycles that could go quite quickly by the standards of the times: the 600 cc pride of the line to the end of the 1960s, the R69S, could usually better 110 mph with the aid of 42 bhp, and with gear ratios somewhat widely spaced in the local tradition of *Alpen und Autobahnen* could accelerate quite smartly. How much it had in reserve was demonstrated in 1961 when a specially prepared version set new records for 12 and 24 hours in the 750 and 1000 cc classes at Montlhèry. This machine had a Peel dolphin fairing, extra lamps, a tuned engine, extra high gearing, and a riding position tailored for the racing crouch;

OPPOSITE The 900 cm³ R90S, top of the BMW range up to the autumn of 1975, has shown surprising agility in production machine races. Here it displays its underpinnings to good effect while cranking through a Brands Hatch corner.

BELOW The Rennsport BMW of 1958 was considered the most powerful and (in a straight line) potentially the fastest racer of the time, but handling problems prevented even Duke, Dale and Anderson from achieving any real success with it.

87

but to a surprisingly large extent it was perfectly standard, ridden by an English team comprising Sid Mizen, George Catlin, John Holder and Ellis Boyce, and it contrived to average over 109 mph including all pit stops. The performance was there, and so (as contemporary road tests reported with some awe) were the brakes necessary to check it. Yet something was missing, something that prevented us from thinking of the BMW as having any sporting appeal.

The handling gave a clue. It was fine on long steady-state bends, but not a machine for twitching along a winding by-road. The ride was soft, well damped, so comfortable as to impart no clue as to the nature of the road surface, while the steering conspired with the suspension to keep the rider ignorant of this vital factor. This remoteness, this desensitization, was everywhere: all those beautifully made controls – the forged levers, the geared twistgrip, even the petrol tap – had none of the feel that one expects in well-bred machinery. It was the triumph of cerebration over sensation.

It was as though one were to civilize a rifle by dulling its hair-trigger. Presumably the action had to be honed again when used for competition, though one suspects that when BMWs succeeded in long-distance production machine races (and indeed they scored some notable successes in the 1950s, including the 500 miles race at Thruxton and the 24 hours event at Barcelona) they did so more by virtue of their stamina than through any superiority of speed or handling. Yet it seems somehow irrelevant: the BMW, even the avowedly sports version which was the R69S, was far too replete in middle-class respectability to indulge in such caperings. It was the machine on which the successful dynamic German businessman would find expression up and down the main road on a Sunday morning, before repeating the journey in the afternoon as the worthy industrious German paterfamilias, driving his household in a Mercedes-Benz. It was a machine for epic journeys, for earnest touring: and it was a matter of entirely personal opinion whether or not it were a fault that it should go like the wind without any bravado whatsoever. It was more a tribute to BMW engineering than to BMW taste that even the R69S, with its stifling silencers and sober city black-and-stripes, would render tame the most uproarious road-burning riders. It was far too civilized, you see: the shaft-drive showed this clearly enough, while one would sooner expect a surgeon's scalpel-hand to shake than that this massive flat-twin should betray its faintly *désaxé* asymmetry by even a tremor – though the rear main bearing of the R69S engine was designed to accommodate crankshaft flexure, which is a sobering thought.

Devon lanes are not like Brands Hatch, but author LJKS enjoys cranking a BMW R75/6 into a left-hander too.

This quality of civilization is one that is difficult to define, but the art historian Sir Kenneth Clark has made an interesting attempt. 'Civilization means something more than energy and will and creative power . . . briefly, a sense of permanence.' In a world of automotive ephemera, permanence means a lot. BMW have acquired their mastery of motorcycle building by steadily applying basic skills and native flair to a set of fundamental problems that have never really changed since they began building in 1920. The firm was founded in 1917, and enjoyed from the outset a fine reputation for its lightweight high-compression aero-engines. After the Great War it obviously had to do something else, and anybody who saw their men carefully studying and sketching Granville Bradshaw's ABC in 1919 might have formed a shrewd idea of what that something else was to resemble.

Before the idea took shape on the drawing boards of founder Max Friz, motorcycle production had already begun with a bijou runabout nicknamed the Flink, and some flat-twin Helios motorcycles with cylinders set longitudinally in the frame, built in the original Munich factory. Then in 1923 came what we could still call the modern BMW as a complete *Gestalt*, with its transverse flat-twin engine and shaft-drive setting the pattern for the next fifty-three years – or, such is the esteem in which the make is currently held, even more. Telescopic fork came in 1935, a sprung rear wheel later in the same decade. Swinging fork front and rear suspension (the former license-built after the pattern of the English Earles) were introduced in the 1950s, with telescopics returning to the front at the end of the 1960s. In each case, after the first novelty had worn off, one hardly noticed the difference. Permanence is the thing.

BSA Gold Star

Way back in the spacious days of Brooklands they used to award a gold star to anyone who lapped the oval concrete Outer Circuit at over 100 mph in a race. The late Walter Handley collected one in July 1937, riding a new 500 cc BSA that lapped at 107.5; and in doing so he founded a dynasty.

He also started something of a furore, for BSA were supposed to be opposed to racing, an opposition painfully established in 1921 when they entered six machines for the Senior TT and all six retired. From that fateful day onwards, no factory BSA had ever raced until Handley broke the tradition of sixteen years standing. Later in 1937 the reason for this apparent change of heart became clear: BSA were producing a new sports model which private owners could buy and race, though the firm themselves had no intention of embarking on an official racing programme. Inevitably, the new machine was the Gold Star.

It was remarkable for two things. One was the use of light alloy for cylinder head and barrel, an outstanding innovation among quantity-production motor-cycles. It was a doubly remarkable feature, for the machine that Handley rode at Brooklands a few months earlier had the iron barrel and head from an earlier engine design – not that it mattered at Brooklands where it was running on alcohol. The other thing about the production Gold Star was that its frame and forks were no better than those of the cheap bread-and-butter machines upon which the prevailing reputation of BSA was founded, and although the machine was undoubtedly fast, it did not handle particularly well. In consequence, it made no discernible impact on the racing scene, though it became popular and successful as a trials mount; and in the early post-war years this involvement with rough country was continued, the addition of telescopic front forks improving the production bicycle's behaviour considerably. In 1948 the Gold Star was reintroduced with light alloy engine, a 350 capable of producing 24 bhp. Moreover, it acquired a sprung heel of plunger type; and since to this basically satisfactory specification were added all the options of tune and equipment that could turn the basic roadster into a road racer, perfectly adapted to the regulations and requirements of clubman's events, it immediately became very popular. No fewer than thirty were entered in the Junior Clubman's TT of 1949; but a motorcycle race is not one of those contests that can be won by campaigning like a Chinese army, and the fact that a Gold Star did win, at over 75 mph, was due not to statistical probability but to the really competitive nature of the machine.

It is not common for motorcycle manufacturers to succeed in thus making a silk purse out of a sow's ear. It was, however, with uncommon imagination that BSA pursued this objective, retaining as many parts of the standard road machine as possible but making alternative apparatus that could convert the basic fast tourer into a trials machine, a scrambler or a road racer. In all three branches of the sport, the Gold Star was to establish for many years the stan-dards by which other machines were judged, remaining competitive for a particularly long time in scrambles. It was as a clubman's racer that it became

The forward setting of the pedals reveals that this 1960 Gold Star no longer serves as a Clubman's racer, and the modern Amal Concentric carburettor is not original; but the rest is as impressive as ever.

The comments in the previous caption apply again, with touring handlebars explaining the alterations. To be fair, the Goldie could be ordered in touring trim – but it hardly ever was.

a classic, however, and when adapted to this function it looked the part to perfection. The straight-through exhaust pipe was not especially remarkable, though it bore evidence of some significant modifications within the engine; and the closeness of the gear ratios had to be heard rather than seen. Rearset footrests, a reversed gear pedal, special brake and kickstarter pedals, alloy wheels, racing seats, all sorts of things were catalogued, enabling this pushrod machine to overcome its humble birth and outpace the race-bred International Norton which everyone had supposed would be its superior.

In the following year, BSA succumbed to the obvious temptation to build a 500 cc version, but this took a lot longer to overcome the Nortons in Senior Clubman's events. In 1951 the engines were redesigned in detail, and in the

following year the new version was raced in a frame which had acquired pivoted-fork rear suspension, grafted to a duplex tube assembly, which was later to become standard on all large BSAs. The combined effect of these changes was to make the Gold Star a superbly controllable motorcycle, one which could at last give the Senior International Norton models a real fight. This was demonstrated rather vividly by W.E. Dow, a novice in road racing, although he had plenty of first-class trials experience on Gold Stars as an Army officer. His performance in the Isle of Man during the Senior Clubman's event was meteoric, for he was fastest in practice, shattered the four-year-old lap record of Geoff Duke in the race, and then fell off rather comprehensively.

It was enough to convince BSA that the 500 was worthy of development, and former Rudge exponent Roland Pike was given the task. His work produced a new engine with much more extensive finning and major re-proportioning of the internals, much attention being given to the valvegear and overall an insistence on careful preparation and the best available materials. The 500 was giving 37 bhp, the 350 30 bhp, and with further attention to the bicycle parts (most notably the clip-on handlebars which were soon to be emulated by so many other firms) the Gold Star was virtually unbeatable. It filled the leader boards in the Junior and Senior Clubman's TT races, was entered in surprisingly large numbers and ridden with respectable results in both larger classes of the TT proper, and in lesser club events up and down the country it simply had no real equivalent against which to compete.

This did not stop development going on, for Pike's engine work continued unabated, ensuring more power as well as even greater reliability. Gold Stars generally finished their races in notably good conditions. Dow won the 1955 Senior Clubman's TT, checked the machine over in a cursory sort of way, and ran it with the same tyres and chains in the Thruxton 9-hour race, which it also won.

Development work continued, but to dominate the opposition was not enough: BSA wanted to paralyze it. In 1956 the Gold Star sported a light alloy fuel tank, a full-width front brake, and the biggest racing carburettor that Amal could furnish. Silencers were mandatory, so Pike devised a combined megaphone and silencer whose shape became a model for imitation by others. The power of the 500 rose to 42 bhp at 7000 rpm, and in its class the machine was as unbeatable as the 350 had been for so long. Paralysis in the opposition was now almost complete: 63 of 68 entrants for the Junior Clubman's events and 31 of 42 for the Senior elected to ride the BSA models, and those who did not could not have been serious. If one wanted to win the race, one simply had to buy the Gold Star, designed and built with the winning of that race most in mind.

The results were a foregone conclusion. Alas, it was all too predictable: as so often happens in racing, complete domination of an event by one make led to a general loss of interest and support. Clubman's racing was stopped: the official announcement was supported by explanations that 1957 would be Golden Jubilee year for the TT, and the organizational resources of the governing body would be too severely taxed. It is natural for official excuses to be framed in such terms, just as it was natural for the tongue-waggers to blame BSA for killing the event by campaigning too earnestly. It would have been fairer to blame other manufacturers for being so half-hearted and lackadaisical in the development of their clubman's machines, whose origins were no more humble and lacklustre than those of the Gold Star. But BSA had to bow to the inevitable, and in 1957 they ceased production of the 350. The 500, however, was still doing very well in scrambles, and the demand for the Gold Star in clubman's trim continued in strength, and so superb was it as a road machine that many were those who delighted to bask in the glory that remained attached to its name. The Gold Star was not a loss-leader, trickled out by the dozen for publicity purposes, but a substantial production item, one or two thousand being built each year; but this was a small figure by BSA standards, and when the touring single-cylinder machines upon which the competition models were based went out of production, its days were numbered. The last Gold Star left the factory in 1964.

Small figures by BSA standards? . . . When the 'Goldie' was involved, the figures were often implausible. There can be very few instances indeed of a vehicle manufacturer publishing horsepower figures that were actually lower than his engines generated (Bristol have been known to do it, but I can think of no others), but BSA were deliberately modest where the Gold Star's bhp were involved. Presumably they meant to lull the opposition into a state of ill-founded confidence, though most of their rivals were afflicted by such engineering and managerial torpor that any additional lullaby would have been a work of supererogation. One of them, at least, was sufficiently bemused by the performance of the big Brummagem single to find out what lay behind it: Eddie Withers of Douglas obtained a 350 Gold Star simply to find out what it was that propelled Eddie Dow so rapidly. When the BSA engine was checked on a dynamometer, it produced much more power than its makers ever claimed. Was it not Charles Turley who wrote that 'Modesty can be cultivated until it becomes something very like a crime?'

Would the Gold Star have seemed less surprisingly high-class had it come from a less plebeian background? Other BSAs were always rather workaday affairs.

H. P. Muller rode Baumm 2 at
Bonneville.

NSU -Baumm

The first NSU car shared its natal year 1906 not only with that classic of conservatism, the Rolls-Royce Silver Ghost, but also with that notorious expression of radicalism, Einstein's *General Theory of Relativity*. Since that time, NSU cars and motorcycles have variously exhibited orthodoxy and heterodoxy in periods of roughly equal duration: the former presumably gave them fewer headaches, but the latter gave them worldwide fame.

That fame had originally been sought way back in 1873 in the manufacture of another kind of technical innovation, namely knitting machines. By 1886 the factory set up in Neckarsulm was making pedal cycles; and when, four years later, something else came out of Neckarsulm – the three letters NSU which were adopted as a brand name – it was well enough known to be worth exploiting when the firm began building motorcycles. This was in 1900, just before the basic shape of the modern motorcycle was established by the New Werner with which this book began. The NSU designs could accordingly be dismissed as mere motorized bicycles; but however the firm might diversify itself in the next sixty-nine years, until the company was taken over in a complicated deal that linked them with Audi (lately the vassals of Daimler-Benz) in subjection to Volkswagen, they never forgot their interest in powered two-wheelers; and there were many occasions when their rivals were not allowed to forget, either.

Indeed there was a period, between the sale of their Heilbronn works to Fiat in 1929 and their resumption of the business in 1958, when (despite the distinction of having produced three prototypes of the KdF Volkswagen under the direction of Dr Ferdinand Porsche) their speciality in the decades immediately before and after the World War was motorcycles.

The resurgence of the German automotive industry under the National Socialist regime has been well enough chronicled, in particular the encourage-

RIGHT Bearded Gustav Adolf Baumm settles into his 'Flying Hammock' on the Munich–Ingolstadt *Autobahn* in May 1955, before setting 22 new world records in various capacity classes. The engines used were the Wankel-supercharged 50 cm³ Quickly moped and the 125 cm³ Rennfox, reaching speeds up to 93.6 and 134.2 mph respectively.

The engine of the NSU 125 Rennfox began life with 15.5 bhp in 1953, rising to 16.8 during the 1954 season. Study of the general layout of the 1954 racer, including its engine, spine frame, front suspension, and exhaust system, may encourage some interesting speculation on the origin of the Honda CB92 design. Relating the power output of the NSU engine to the speed of the Baummwagen it propelled may be even more enlightening.

The over-the-counter NSU racer for privateers was the single-cylinder 250 cm³ Sportmax, equally closely related to roadsters and works racers.

ment given to Auto-Union and Daimler-Benz by the Nazi government to embark on a lavish racing programme as a public relations exercise on an international scale. The same thing applied, albeit on a more modest scale and a more straitened budget, to motorcycles. Thus in 1935, after only two years under the Chancellorship of Hitler, a very interesting motorcycle show at Berlin included a promising pair of overhead-camshaft NSU racers. By 1939, NSU had caught the supercharging bug that promised to infect the whole sport, and they offered a substantial challenge to the opposition in the 350 cc class in 1939 with a supercharged parallel twin. It was perhaps too substantial: the machine weighed nearly 50 lb more than the BMW works 500 racer, and was burdened by another 50 lb of fuel to slake its immoderate thirst. Nevertheless it provided the engineering basis for a run of motorcycles that after the War were to be immensely successful.

It was ten years before production could be resumed after the ravages of the war, but within another two years Wilhelm Herz was riding a blown 500 cc NSU at 180 mph to take the absolute world speed record for motorcycles. The supercharged NSU was a prodigious performer in domestic race meetings, where the Germans still revelled in supercharging; but in international events forced induction was banned, and it was confidently assumed that the leadership in unblown engines asserted by Norton in the 1920s would remain with the British for years to come. NSU set about making unsupercharged engines for international racing at the highest level, however, and came up with a design that must have been one of the most scientifically devised of the era. The bicycle part itself was beautiful enough, exquisitely made and superbly detailed in its backbone frame, vast brakes and streamlined fairing. More important, it boasted an engine that in terms of volumetric efficiency was without peer. The Rennsport NSU was the first, and for a long time the only, unblown motor developing 125 bhp per litre. In 250 and 125 cc categories these twin-overhead-camshaft twin-cylindered machines brought NSU the world championships on at least four occasions – and incidentally furnished the technical inspiration for the first serious high-grade Honda motorcycles.

In common with several other firms, NSU pulled out of motorcycle racing in the mid-1950s (their brilliant team leader Werner Haas was killed in a flying accident in 1956) and, although their sporting motorcycles remained in production for some time thereafter, they became best known for their mopeds, the NSU Quickly at one time enjoying an enormous vogue. As though to lend weight to their marketing campaign they embarked on a series of record-breaking sessions with a most extraordinary motorcycle, a slim, low, cigar-like projectile known as Gustav Baumm's Flying Hammock.

The major component of the resistance offered by a motorcycle to the propulsion offered by its engine is its aerodynamic drag, which is a function of the vehicle's shape and of its frontal area. When high speeds are sought it is therefore logical to reduce the frontal area as much as is possible and at the same time to refine the shape until it penetrates the air as cleanly as possible. The pursuit of these two not wholly compatible ideals to the point of logical extremity was the ideal of Gustav Baumm, a bearded but youthful scientist whose expression of his faith in his creation was to ride it.

To do so he had to lie supine, cabinned, cribbed and confined within its aluminium carapace, and peering out through a small transparent canopy. The handlebars were in the only place where there was space for them, beneath his knees; and they were linked to the hub-centre steering mechanism with which, by elimination of the conventional steering head, it was possible to keep the overall height of the vehicle so low. Behind him was a tiny NSU engine which somehow sufficed to propel this admittedly ultrarefined aerodyne at enormous speeds. The most extraordinary result of all was with the smallest engine: on the Bonneville salt flats in Utah, the Baumm streamliner shattered the 50 cc record with a speed of 121.9 mph.

A great deal more might have been expected of this incomparably elegant bicycle; but as with so many other pioneers of truly modern transport, from Otto Lilienthal (remember his last words – 'Sacrifices must be paid for.') to Geoffrey de Havilland, Fate exacted her payment in advance. Attempting to go even faster, Baumm left the road and crashed fatally. Truly there was no need for him to try any harder, for he had already proved the truth that he was so zealous to assert; and there can be no doubt that most of the credit for the results he achieved belongs to the aerodynamics of his streamlined challenge to dicyclic orthodoxy. The 50 cc record was taken with an engine giving only 12.8 bhp; but that, from what was tantamount to a well-made moped engine, was equivalent to 256 bhp per litre.

NSU were very careful to keep quiet about the inconspicuous supercharger that gave this machine its outstanding performance, a belt-driven supercharger which could deliver air to the engine at pressures up to 8 atmospheres ($120 \, lb/in^2$) with an overall adiabatic efficiency exceeding 70% and therefore comparable with the best aero-engine compressors. In fact, for the record the boost pressure was limited to $45 \, lb/in^2$, and this sufficed to increase the power output of the NSU Quickly engine (which was of course suitably modified) by a factor of about 8. The reason for the secrecy was not simply the high boost pressure but the manner in which it had so efficiently been attained: the supercharger was an early prototype of what was to become the Wankel engine, and was to bring NSU enormous fame and crippling problems.

The first contract between NSU and Felix Wankel had been in 1951, when their head of research – the brilliant and witty Dr Ing. Walter Froede – wanted information about the sealing arrangements for some rotary valves that had preoccupied Wankel during the war. Wankel had used rotary disc valves for torpedo engines; Froede wanted to do the same for a racing motorcycle. The agreement into which Wankel and NSU entered was originally aimed only at this particular sealing problem; but as time passed their ideas enjoyed fissile development. It was early in 1954 that Wankel realized how the four-stroke cycle could be enveloped by an epitrochoidal bore containing an equilateral rotor. It was 1956 when a compressor based on Wankel's idea boosted the engines of Baumm's record-breaker. A year later, Froede had accomplished the intellectual feat of turning the relative motions of the rotating inner and outer members of this machine inside out, to create the simple definitive single-rotor Wankel engine as we know it, and to some extent understand it, today.

ABOVE Werner Haas on the 1953 NSU 250 Rennmax.

LEFT The resurgence of the German motorcycle industry as a source of competitive machinery dates from the encouragement and inducements offered to industry by the publicity-conscious Nazi regime. By 1935 there was already something for Hitler to be shown.

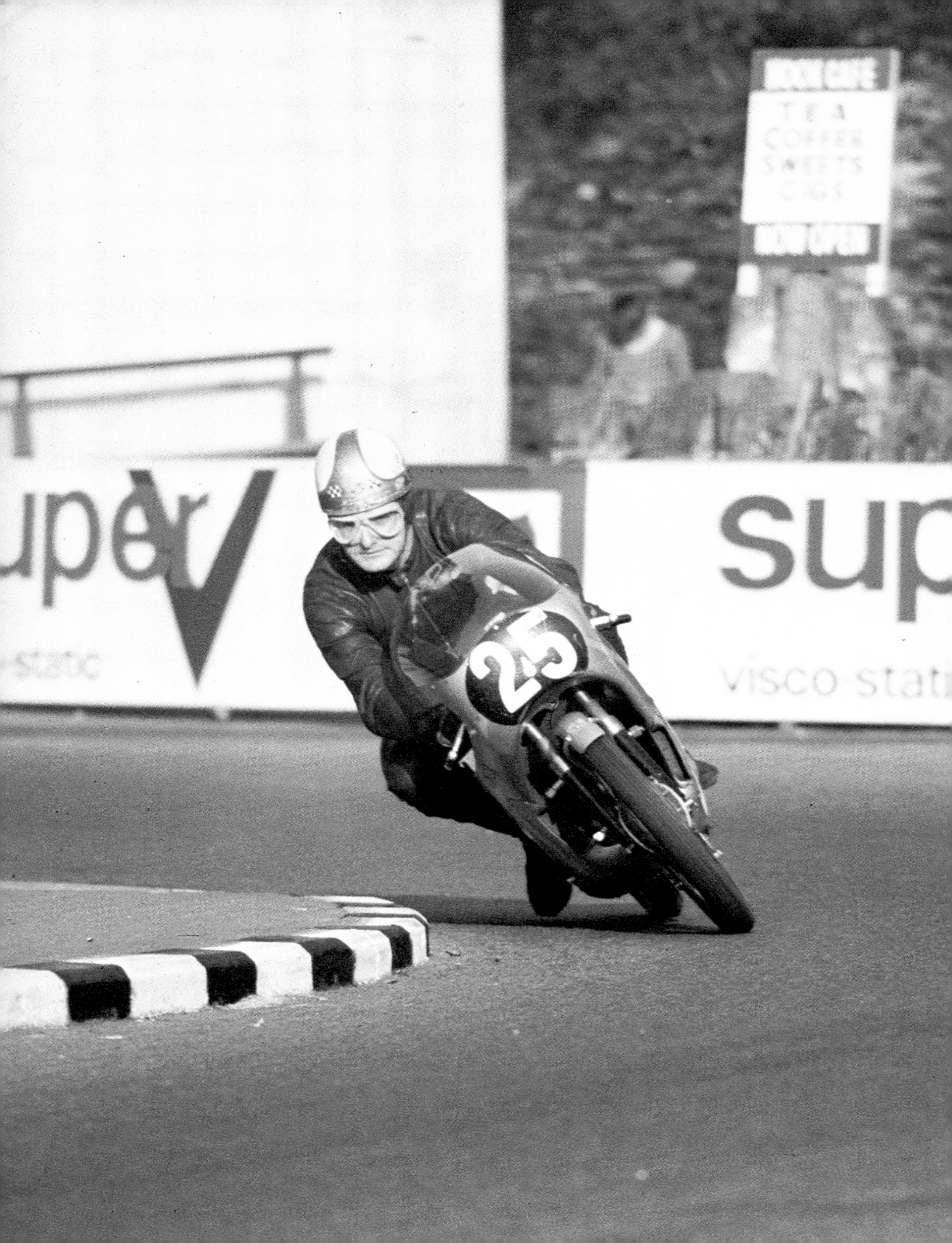
TEA
COFFEE
SWEETS
CIGS
NOW OPEN
sup
visco-stati

Honda Benly Super Sport

'He that contemneth small things', wrote Ecclesiasticus 'shall fall by little and little.' It was by little initial steps that Honda grew from 1950 to become the largest motorcycle producer in the world, raping with comparatively little machines the markets that hitherto existed apparently for the benefit of much larger engined British and European motorcycles. It was likewise in quite a small way that Honda first ventured into serious motorcycle racing, sending a team of five weeny 125 cc bicycles to run in the 1959 TT. One of these retired, and the remainder finished sixth, seventh, eighth, and eleventh to win the manufacturers' team prize. In the following year they did a little more and a little better, finishing in sixth to tenth places inclusive in the 125 class and sending an amazing four-cylinder 250 to pursue the MV Agusta duo of Hocking and Ubbiali and the Morini ridden by the dashing Provini, and to finish fourth in the hands of Brown.

It had never occurred to anybody that a motorcycle engine might run up to 14,000 rpm, still less that a 250 might have four cylinders – although Guzzi had produced a superb V8 500 some years earlier, making the idea less unreasonable – but when Honda then produced a four-cylinder 125 which shrilled up to 18,000 rpm, the playboys of the western world threw up their hands in despair. It was no longer any use dismissing the micro-cylindered oriental machines as too remote to be of consequence and too small to be of interest. It was very nearly too late to dispel the old diehard notion that a good big 'un would always beat a good little 'un, even when that great rider McIntyre had expressed the current state of affairs by explaining that he was faster on his Italian 350 cc Bianchi than on his British 500 Norton, and faster still on his 250 Honda. It was too late to stop Honda winning the world championships in the 125, 250 and 350 classes by 1962, and too late also for the European manufacturers to check the disaffection of their customers, who were deserting their bluff and brawny companions of the road in favour of these more pointedly elegant, suave and far from pusillanimous orientals.

And so we began to see, amid a sprinkling of two-strokes that were soon to grow into a flood, lightweight machines like the Honda Benly demonstrating to the reactionary British manufacturers in particular that mass production and competitive prices were not incompatible with multiple cylinders, overhead camshafts, and electric starters. Electric starters? To listen to the manufacturers of the motorcycles that needed them more than any, there ought to have been sumptuary laws proscribing them.

Yet the CB92 Benly Super Sport, for all the rakishness of its looks, was sumptuously equipped. Apart from the generosity of the electrical system, the brakes would have done justice to a far heavier and faster machine: they were each 8 inches in diameter, the front having two leading shoes, and the total lining area of 41 square inches was 12% greater than that of the Vincent Black

Greatest of all riders, S. M. B. Hailwood practising for the TT on a 125 Honda in 1966, the year in which the Japanese factory produced a five-cylinder engine for this ultra-lightweight class.

Shadow which was 200 lb heavier and 50 mph faster. The Vincent, to be fair, had a reputation for good braking; the little Honda was braked like a racer.

Not only in its brakes – and in its looks, which echoed those of the original racing venturers three or four years earlier – but also in its power characteristics was it like a racer. The engine's maximum output was realized at 10,500 rpm when it amounted to about 15 bhp; but the peak of the torque curve was little lower at 9000 rpm, and very little happened at all below 5000. So to get the best of the little Honda's performance, or indeed to get much performance at all, it was imperative to keep the thing in the uppermost 25% of the range (it was safe to 12,000), in which exercise the spacing of the gear ratios – 1, 1.23, 1.74, and 2.8 to 1 – was barely close enough and certainly not ideal, though it repre-

BELOW The Honda Benly Super Sport was more than an exquisite motorcycle: it was also a superb piece of industrial design, significantly better in almost every detail and more attractive overall than the racing NSU by which it was so clearly inspired.

RIGHT The art of the miniaturist was never so well exemplified as by the lightweight multi-cylinder Honda engines of the 1960s. The early racing 125 twin was no exception: this exploded drawing of the cylinder head assembly only becomes a thing at which to wonder when the dimensions are taken into account.

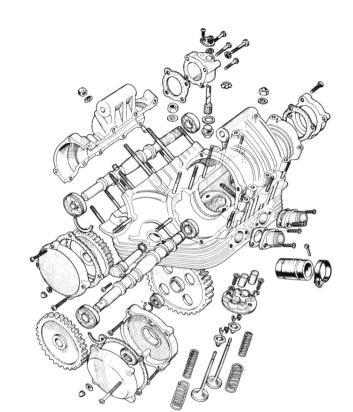

sented a fair compromise between conflicting demands. But the engine itself showed what could be achieved when conventional restraints were cast aside, and designers could feel free to pursue almost *ad absurdum* the reasoning of the late L.H. Pomeroy, who observed in 1910 'Revolutions are of an abstract nature; they cost nothing, weigh nothing, have no shape or substance. If one can achieve more revolutions than another, it is hard to find a reason why he should not benefit thereby.'

Never was this so truly taken to heart as by Honda designers in the early 1960s. Extrapolating from their two-cylinder 50 cc racer, they produced for the 1966 season a 125 whose engine carried five cylinders in line athwartships, its crankshaft spinning with apparent imperturbability up to 23,000 rpm. It was an incredible engine, in which detonation simply could not be induced with petrol of as little as 80 octane anti-knock rating, and could only be induced below about 15,000 rpm on petrol that was of less than 70 octane rating. This machine was to dominate its class and to win its appropriate world championship; but almost more significantly it was to inspire the international presentation of a technical paper by Honda engineers in which they demonstrated that virtually all the problems of petrol engine design and construction disappear at over 10,000 rpm.

There were other designers insistent at the time of the CB92's introduction – and there still are today – that revolutions are but the calf of gold and thou shalt have none other God but volumetric efficiency. Yet Honda did not do too badly on this score, with 153 lb/in² peak bmep from the Benly Super Sport engine whose compression ratio at 10 : 1 was by no means unreasonable for such small cylinders, whose stroke : bore ratio of 0.93 : 1 was entirely fashionable for the time, and whose single carburettor was downright modest in its very singularity.

It was a pity that, despite all this engineeering virtuosity and styling brilliance, Honda could not contrive better handling than they did. To make any road vehicle handle well is still accounted more an art than a science, and a black art at that; and it is one in which Honda have often been accused of being deficient. In the Benly's case it is probable that the fault lay in an unhappy choice of spring rates and damper settings; but Honda chose after a few more years to abandon the pressed steel backbone frame, the generously boxed and stiffened trailing rear forks and blade type front forks with their bottom link suspension (all derived from the once very successful NSU lightweights which had seemed objects well worthy of emulation) and switched to tubular frames and telescopic front forks. The new ones looked singularly devoid of inspiration, but the customers kept turning up and the new vogue of motorcycles for the millions was firmly established.

In his first twenty business years Honda sold 10 million motorcycles, most of them with tiny engines, and not a few mere mopeds. Despite the fact that his range today includes such monsters as the 1000 cc Gold Wing, the feel for miniaturization is still evident and it is difficult to say of such a man that he has done it all wrong. Even if you ignore Ecclesiasticus, there is still Zechariah: 'For who hath despised the day of small things?'

ABOVE R. McIntyre still rode a Norton 500 Manx in the early 1960s. He also rode a Bianchi 350 which, he said, was faster – and this Honda 250 which, he continued, was faster still.

LEFT Dr M. R. Wigan, scientist and spare-time motorcycling journalist, loved his Honda 125 racer perhaps more than any other of his many and impressive machines.

MZ racers

And not by eastern windows only
When daylight comes, comes in the light
In front the sun comes slow, how slowly,
But westward, look, the land is bright.

The two-stroke disc valve was invented by Zimmermann, developed by Walter Kaaden, exploited by Ernst Degner, and made the modestly financed MZ team from East Germany the fastest things in their classes. These were the machines that set the modern two-stroke on its frantically powerful, frighteningly unmanageable and dipsomaniacally thirsty way. They might ultimately have done even more, but Degner defected to the West – by going East, to Suzuki and Yamaha, and a new generation of high-output motorcycles that owe volumes to the little pioneers of Zschopau.

From the earliest days of the two-stroke engine, when Clark, Fielding and Robson were working on it around about 1880, it had enjoyed little respect from motorcyclists. The one exception was the decidedly atypical two-stroke engine devised by Alfred Scott in 1898; but his fertile intellect seemed able to conjure up a magic that few others could understand and scarcely any could emulate. None of the numerous advances made subsequently by Day and Ricardo and Dunelt and so on made much difference, not even the deflectorless-piston loop-scavenge system of Dr Schnuerle whose ideas were adopted enthusiastically by DKW in the 1930s. Any two-stroke motorcycle that was not a Scott could automatically be dismissed as a futilitarian potterer – until people started supercharging two-strokes, when the situation changed dramatically. Supercharging made especially good sense when allied with the split-single two-strokes that had been pioneered by Puch, because the asymmetric motions of the two pistons allowed the port timings in their siamesed cylinders to convert what would otherwise be a mere scavenging air-flow into a genuine boost: that is, the exhaust port could be closed before the inlet port. DKW, who had pinned their faith on supercharging as early as 1925 when they started racing, took up the blown split-single in 1931, and by the end of the decade they were fielding a racing 250 the enormity of whose performance was only excelled by a fuel thirst that strained credulity and a noise that defied description.

Things could not hope to be the same after the World War. In the first place, DKW had to reconstitute themselves (as part of the Auto Union group) in Ingolstadt, because their original factory at Zschopau was in Russian-occupied East Germany; and in the second place the supercharging of racing motorcycles was no longer allowed. The old factory resumed motorcycle manufacture, however, and the title VEB Motorradwerk Zschopau established in 1946 the initials MZ which were a dozen years later to strike something like terror into those riders in the 125 and 250 racing classes who had supposed they would continue to dominate events with motorcycles bearing the initials MV.

In charge of the MZ racing department was Walter Kaaden, an engineer whose revaluation of the two-stroke concept confirmed him as a genius. Starting

in 1953 with a 125 cc engine employing the crankshaft-driven rotary disc valve
that had been invented and patented by Zimmerman, Kaaden soon realized
that it was a mistake to treat the two-stroke engine as all previous exponents had
treated it, as a pump whose piston induced and expelled air and combustion
gases. An engine did not have to have any moving parts in order to induce such
a flow: aviation scientists, perhaps spurred on by the very simple flap-valve
reaction jet engine of the war-time German V1 flying bomb, were experimenting with the athodyd – or aero-thermodynamic duct – through which gas flow
and combustion could be sustained with no moving parts whatever, simply
by putting the whole variable-section pipe (which is all that the athodyd
amounted to) into resonance and adding energy in the form of combustible
fuel at the critical point. Kaaden saw the two-stroke engine as a kind of athodyd,
a resonant system that would maintain gas flow in just the same way, the only
difference being that instead of harnessing propulsive effort by reaction against
a fast-moving jet efflux, it was done by reaction against the piston of what was
still a basically simple reciprocating engine. His thermodynamic duct com-
prised a short but highly resonant induction tract, whose timing was controlled
by a rotary disc with a cut-away section that allowed it a long opening period
that could be determined independently of the opening and closure of the
piston-controlled ports in the cylinder wall, some of which were transfer ports,
while the exhaust port communicated with the independently resonant exhaust
pipe.

If one is a particularly clever engineer, as Kaaden was, it would be possible
to reach a first approximation for the dimensions of the system by means of

TOP Ubbiali (MV Agusta) stays ahead
of Degner (MZ) in the 250 GP des
Nations at Monza in 1959.

ABOVE The bald-crowned man busy
with watch and lapscore is MZ's Walter
Kaaden, the father of modern two-
stroke technology.

Peter Williams coaxes a 250 MZ around the soaking Dundrod circuit for the Ulster GP.

laborious calculations taking account of gas temperature, mass flow, the coefficients of discharge of the various ports, and everything else from atmospheric pressure and humidity to the colour of the rider's eyes. Kaaden did this for a start, but it was only a start: thereafter it was a matter of laborious experiment, a suck-it-and-see procedure in which too often the answer was a lemon.

Kaaden's perseverance gradually bore fruit. The power of his engines grew steadily, and was boosted dramatically when he devised a divergent-convergent exhaust pipe that not only resonated to suck the vitiated products of combustion out of the cylinder when the exhaust port was uncovered, but also timed a high-pressure pulse to travel in the opposite direction and ram the following fresh scavenging mixture back into the cylinder just before the exhaust port closed again. By 1961 Kaaden was rewarded with the first unsupercharged engine to yield 200 bhp per litre, in a single-cylinder machine that was the fleetest 125 in existence.

For some years the MZ had already been highly competitive in the lightweight and ultra-lightweight classes, threatening to topple the crowns of the MV Agusta four-strokes that in those days ruled the roost as autocratically as the four-cylinder 'fire engines' of the same make did in the Junior and Senior classes. The MZ was blisteringly fast, of that there was no doubt; but it was also terribly temperamental, as sore a trial to its riders as to its rivals. Early handling

Earles forks did nothing to help the handling of this early 125 MZ.

problems were overcome by the simple stratagem of fitting Norton front forks (not replicas but the genuine articles), but the mercurial moods of the engine were more difficult to manage. A change in the barometer, such as a four-stroke might shrug off, would give the highly tuned two-stroke a fit of the sulks; a fatigue-induced split in an exhaust pipe, that might merely lop off the peak of a four-stroke's power curve, would demolish that of the MZ completely – though to tell the truth its power curve consisted only of a peak, since the precious resonance could only be effective over an extremely narrow band of revolutions, making its close-ratio six-speed gearbox as necessary an adjunct as a really precise rider. The consumption of fuel was very heavy, and the consumption of little-end bearings almost as bad. Self-appointed critics also poured scorn on the rearward-facing exhaust ports, pronouncing that this disposition must have made the barrels hotter in the port area than if they had faced in the opposite direction; but Kaaden was one of those East European engineers who were particularly well-versed in the niceties of air-cooled engine design, and who generally espoused the doctrine of the brilliant Tatra engineer Julius Mackerle who had pointed out that air-cooling depended on the temperature gradient between fins and air, so that if the cooling air flow impinged first on the hot side of the cylinder, it would grow too hot to do any good by the time it got round to the other side, whereas if it started work on the cooler side it would

be only mildly warm by the time it had reached around to the hot spot and thus still capable of effective heat abstraction.

For all its petty troubles, the MZ with 25 bhp from the 125 cc engine and something like 48 from the 250 (which was simply a brace of 125s set back to back, their crankshafts coupled into a common take-off gear), was extremely effective; and in 1961 the East German flyer looked a certainty to win the ultra-lightweight world championship. The firm's real trouble was not with machinery but with money: they could never engage star riders because they were unable to pay them. When Gary Hocking had ridden the 125 and 250 two-strokes to a dominating position in the 1960 world championships, all MV Agusta had to do was to wave a bag of gold under his nose and he was gone. Hailwood, Shepherd, Williams, and Taveri, all of them brilliant riders who occasionally strove on MZ's behalf, all said the same thing: they would have been very happy to remain in the team, if only its organization had not been hampered by a shoestring budget which allowed them nothing. The only regular MZ rider was Ernst Degner, and he was undoubtedly very good. He was more than just a brilliant rider, and if he did not have the engineering stature of the creative Walter Kaaden he did at least fully comprehend the new science of two-stroke tuning and was himself an adept practitioner of it.

Heinz Rosner on a 250 MZ at Brands Hatch in 1966.

INSET MZ racers were never paragons of reliability, but this 250 was one of only eight machines to finish a Lightweight TT in which 64 started. Ridden by the superbly stylish Alan Shepherd, it finished second to the factory Honda of Jim Redman.

Such a man was very precious to the team, especially towards the end of the 1961 season when he led his nearest rival in the 125 cc championship by two points with only one race to go. That race was the Argentine GP, but Degner was not allowed to take part in it: he had chosen the occasion to seek asylum while out of his native country, and while the politicians and diplomats debated his defection his racing licence was suspended, allowing the title to go by default to Honda rider Tom Phillis.

MZ struggled on a little longer, without any improvement either in their resources or their luck. Meanwhile Degner, now a confirmed extrapatriate, went to Japan and sold his science and skills to Suzuki. The Japanese firm had been getting nowhere with conventional two-strokes, but with Degner's aid their fortunes changed rapidly. After a lot of development and a little water-cooling, first Suzuki and then Yamaha showed the world what wonders could be wrought when Kaaden's ideas were backed by thorough and unstinted support. It had been a long struggle – and though Degner probably never read the lines by Arthur Hugh Clough which headed this chapter, he might have appreciated the title under which they were originally written: 'Say not the struggle naught availeth.'

Dunstall Atlas

Dunstall's 750 Dominator in the hands
of Croxford in the 1968 Thruxton 500-
mile production race.

It is recorded of Sir Joseph Banks that he refused to go on Captain Cook's second voyage because he would not be allowed to have two horn players making music for him during dinner. One sees his point, of course: there are some things of which two are so manifestly better than one as to make one intolerable. Motorcyclists were to feel the same about cylinders in the mid-1950s when Norton, having withdrawn from the racing in which their classical singles were no longer competent, applied themselves to the development of something simpler, cheaper, but at least equally fast to be sold as an over-the-counter production racer. Inevitably the frame and cycle parts had much in common with the featherbed Manx: but the engine was derived from the vertical twin of their road-going Dominator model.

This engine, despite the limitations of pushrod operation of the valves, made good use of the advantages inherent in the multiplicity of cylinders – large piston area, large valve area, light and more easily cooled valves, and an ability to run at high rates of rotation. With the ingredients altered to maintain a racing consistency the recipe worked well enough to produce about 55 bhp at 7600 rpm, making the machine as fast as the overhead-camshaft racer, slightly more accelerative and, perhaps because it carried its weight lower, even better in its handling.

The first of these Domiracers, as they were called, appeared in 1958 and performed convincingly enough. Shortly afterwards, however, the Norton company was taken over by AMC, and most of their Domiracer gear was disposed of to a young and promising short-circuit rider named Paul Dunstall. A proficient tuner, he quickly recognized the advantages of the larger 600 cc Norton for the classes of racing in which he was involved. An amalgam of street and racing machinery, it proved very successful, and other riders began to demand motorcycles of similar classification and performance. Thus the Dunstall Dominator was born, into an age when the custom-built motorcycle was beginning to take the place of the famous classics built by respected but by now largely defunct firms.

It was a paradoxical situation. The motorcycle industry was suffering a slump of crippling severity, and fewer and fewer motorcycles were being bought or ridden; yet the demand for a motorcycle that looked different from all the others was stronger than ever before, and customers proved ready to pay substantially for glamorous and fast machines bespoke-tailored to suit their precisely imagined needs. The ranks of the customizers swelled visibly as the 1960s progressed, most of them dealing mainly in bolt-on equipment that was as much cosmetic as functional. A few went further in building complete motorcycles based more or less on the few remaining quantity-production roadsters worthy of their attention; and of these, Dunstall worked and prospered to such good effect that by 1966 the Board of Trade recognized him as a motorcycle manufacturer in his own right, since he was making more of each machine than the original manufacturer. The ACU, governing body of British motorcycling sport, pursued the same reasoning in accepting the Dunstall Dominator as a make eligible for the 1967 Production TT.

By this time Norton were producing their largest engine yet, the brawny and vibratory 750 cc Atlas. With this engine re-balanced and tuned, and installed

in his regular disc-braked featherbed chassis, Dunstall had a 61 bhp machine of prodigious potential. This was demonstrated by an attack on the one-hour record in the 750 class which, as recorded on page 87, had been established by a BMW (in the course of a 24-hour stint, to be fair) in 1961. The old figure of 111.046 mph was sent toppling when the Dunstall Dominator covered 126.7

Griff Jenkins on the 750 Dunstall Norton with which he failed by a whisker to set new class records for the hour at Monza in 1966. The attempt was hampered by bad weather.

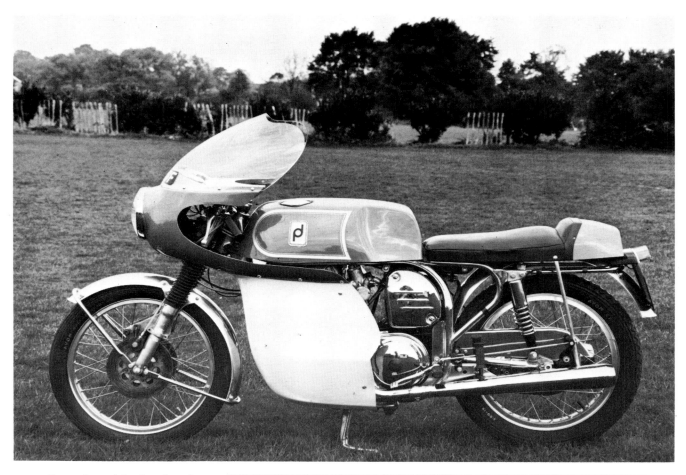

ABOVE Dunstall 750 Atlas, based on the production Norton. The front disc brakes are by Lyster.

RIGHT In 1967 the one-hour record fell to the Dunstall 750 Domiracer at Monza. Rex Butcher rode 10 km at 120.8 mph, 100 km at 126.9, and averaged 126.8 mph for the hour.

miles in the hour at Monza, demolishing en route two records for 10 and 100 kilometres that had stood to the credit of Raleigh and Norton since the late 1920s.

The following year was even more successful, for in 1968 the latest Dunstall proved itself demonstrably the fastest production motorcycle in long-distance racing. Weighing less than 400 lb (more than 50 less than the basic Norton from which it was derived) and developing 67.5 bhp at 6800 rpm, it reached 132.6 mph at the fastest point of the Isle of Man circuit in the course of winning the Production TT. With that same high gearing it mustered acceleration such as would shame a Manx Norton or G50 Matchless; and indeed its winning speed of 98.13 mph was surpassed by only four outright racing motorcycles in the whole of TT Week.

Here then might be seen what was considered in the late 1960s to be the ultimate in man-sized road-burners. It combined titanic power, mercurial mobility, the glamour of Californian hedonism and the rigour of British traditionalism. Advanced technologies were represented by the hydraulically operated disc brakes and by the intriguing exhaust system – the two pipes were coupled by a large-bore balance pipe close to the exhaust ports, downstream of which they were attenuated by 20% in cross-sectional area, developing later into long shallow megaphones containing integral silencers. This type of exhaust system had been first devised by the indefatigible and innovative brain of Doug Hele of Triumph, and proved to amplify flexibility without any sacrifice in peak power – though if the attenuation were omitted, as in production Triumph and BSA machines for some years afterwards, the effect was merely to reduce the noise level.

All this was new and interesting; and if it were remarked that there remained much that was old – that the chassis and engine and controls manifestly had eighteen years behind them and fundamentally were as old as motorcyling itself – then we must conclude, as history seems to suggest, that certain things about motorcycling are commonly considered inalienable and unalterable. All the evidence in this book supports the idea – and whether it be received in sorrow, in anger, or with glee, is an entirely personal matter for every several reader – that designing a desirable motorcycle has not yet been brought down to the level of science, and must therefore still be an art.

Alas! Dunstall was to find, like so many others since, that the typical motor-cyclist had little understanding of science and less appreciation of art. If the motorcycle was to be for him something more than a cheap substitute for shoe leather, it was likely to be as a prop for his declining ego, its appearance entirely dictated by the whims of commercially fermented fashion, so that function became subservient to form – which is an inversion of propriety that neither science nor art can survive. The lure of profitability proved more tempting than the lore of prowess, and as the years went by Dunstall applied his talents increasingly – and successfully – to the marketing of what might be called 'fashion wares' until, ten years after Board of Trade recognition of him as a motorcycle manufacturer, his business had developed and specialized to the point where the manufacture of a motorcycle would be considered an unwelcome chore.

Laverda 750

Machinery and motorcycles mean something very special to Italians. Long years of supremacy in international racing, and decades of unfaltering enthusiasm in national events, have left them convinced that any Italian motorcycle should, as a point of honour, have the air of a mettlesome high-stepping race-proved thoroughbred. For it to be dull would be despicable, if it felt soggy it would be sacrilegious, if it were merely utilitarian it would be an offence against patriotic self esteem.

How romantic – and how illusory! Italy has produced her share – though, to her credit, less than her fair share – of grey porridgey motorcycles, lacklustre loafers that never suffered the foreigners' scorn because they never ventured into the foreigners' ken. At least there were some cases where this traducing of supposed tradition was understandable and therefore forgivable: firms trying to struggle to their feet in the chaos that was Italy after the World War had to earn their living as best they could, and at the same time were morally obliged to offer their customers the sort of basic transport that was all they could hope for and as much as they could afford.

Such was the lot of the brothers Laverda when they established themselves as motorcycle manufacturers in 1949. They concentrated on the commuter market, beginning with a little 75 cc machine. Before long it grew to 100 cc, and by the time the Laverda had grown to a 200 cc twin its name had already gathered considerable prestige earned from successes in the Giro d'Italia – a race that, like the Mille Miglia for cars, was run over a big mileage of ordinary roads, over the breadth and much of the length of Italy, and which therefore put a premium on real roadworthiness as opposed to sheer (or mere) speed. Already the *genius loci* was making its presence felt.

After twenty years of tiddlers the brothers decided to change direction and pace, to move on from the *pasta* to the *panforte*, to establish themselves in the quality market with the sort of high-quality high-performance riding tool that they as passionate riders themselves would like, the sort that they were competent to judge. This was in 1968, at a time when the rest of the Italian motorcycle industry looked unable to climb out of its slough of despond: when Gilera had forgotten all about their fire-engines; when MV Agusta were making little but helicopters; when Guzzi were kept alive only by supply contracts with the army and police. It was a time, in short, when few people would have believed that for the motorcycle industry there were good times just around the corner. In any case it is unlikely that the brothers coldly calculated the prospect of profitability; they did something they had always wanted to do, succumbed to a corpuscular infection they were powerless to resist. Massimo Laverda and the younger Pedro had motorcycle riding in their blood, real hard compulsive and utterly committed riding. If they were invoking anew the languishing spirit of the Italian high-performance motorcycle, that came naturally; if they were creating in the process a machine to make playboys wonder and devoted riders drool, that came naturally too.

Today's three-cylinder Laverda 1000 is as exemplary as the 750 twin was a few years earlier.

Before long, their first offering was going the rounds of such motorcycle shows as Europe still supported. It was a 650 cc twin, and the public's first reaction was to deride it as a gross parody of the Honda CB 77. The engine admittedly did look similar, though it was twice as big: but when people began to look further, they noticed that the castings really were rather beautiful, that the finish of everything was excellent, that the details were carefully thought out and painstakingly executed. Perhaps it would be all right after all.

There was not long to wait. A lot of things were changed, but the basic idea was a good one. With the engine enlarged to 750 cc, the Laverda promptly took its rightful place among the élite of the world's motorcycles. Designed as a highway express, it rapidly proved itself formidable in long-distance racing – naturally, because it was purposely endowed with all the necessary attributes, because it had tremendous power and strength and stamina; because it had marvellous balance and steering; because it had quite exceptional brakes; because – in the best traditions of vehicle manufacture in Northern Italy – there is no other way to make a motorcycle when the factory has the Alps at the back door, and an *autostrada* near the front.

It was not so much a factory, more like a converted country house; but the

ABOVE In production-racing SFC specification, the 750 Laverda was fast, tireless and very well behaved – an Italian successor to some of the traditions of the BSA Clubman's Gold Star, perhaps.

OPPOSITE ABOVE A strong goer and an equally strong stopper, the Laverda 750 displayed fine workmanship throughout.

RIGHT With its engine revised (and no less powerful) to meet new exhaust laws, and with disc brakes producing exceptionally stable stopping power, the later versions of the 750 Laverda became machines of connoisseur quality.

300 men that worked there and in the outbuildings were soon busily producing 7000 motorcycles a year, every one of them spoken for in advance. Whatever the whims and caprices of the retailers, the wholesale price at the factory gates was the same as that of the 750 BMW, and the quality as high as could be found anywhere. Unstinting thoroughness was what ensured that quality, evident in the flawlessness of the castings and forgings, in the finish on all surfaces, and the felicities of countless details such as the click-stop petrol taps, the easy-to-use centre stand, or the generous 24 Ah battery feeding a one-horsepower starter motor. It was confidence, not courage, that prompted the brothers to dispense with a kickstarter pedal.

They stinted on nothing that was desirable. The two-throw crankshaft ran in a total of five bearings, the overhead camshaft in four, and although the engine ought to have been as rough and vibratory as all the other horrid vertical twins, it was not. The cycle parts were well supported too: the crux of the matter, the steering head, was firmly trussed by four frame tubes that came together to form a spine and diverged again behind the engine and gearbox, which were bolted in to complete a very stiff quadrilateral that defied relative movement of the steering head and the rear fork pivot. Every item of the lavish specification was treated with equal thoroughness: each machine was supplied

Lustier and yet lighter than the 750, the Laverda 1000 only disappoints by being more conventional in its frame design.

with two saddles – a dual seat for poodlefaking and a single seat with a racing-style backstop hump which guaranteed that the rider could stay put even if accelerating flat out while wearing PTFE trousers. An interesting refinement was the way that the nose of the seat sloped up to blend into the contours of the usefully big petrol tank: this was to avoid the dangers of castration in emergency stops when those paralyzing brakes were fully exercised. The Laverda brothers think of everything.

No motorcycle so generously endowed could be as light as rivals designed by accountants. The 750 Laverda weighed at least 480 lb, and ready for the road was likely to be well over 500; but it belied its size, responding like a bicycle of much smaller mass, and only a pronounced oversteer when trying to turn tightly at speeds below about 10 mph marred its easy, predictable steering. For the next 110 mph, there were no problems. . . .

The makers claimed 119 mph for the 750 SF that they considered their semi-sporting model. The first one I rode had a speedometer that read 10 mph fast all the way up, but it had real power all the way up, enough on the open road to drive the needle off the end of the 125 mph scale. Success in production and endurance racing had already proved the Laverda sound, but the feel of this elegant muscle-bike on the open road was proof enough.

In touring guise, with drum brakes, the Laverda 750 still has some appeal as a police motorcycle.

Yamaha 350 racer

When, in the 750 cc TT of 1975, Grant on a Kawasaki at last broke the absolute Mountain Circuit lap record that had stood to the credit of Hailwood on a 500 Honda since 1967, it did not do much to make the situation seem any less unreal; but at least it brought matters up to date. We could then con the list of the fastest men and machines around the Island with a better sense of perspective – but the list still contains some surprises. Tenth fastest in the list is Gary Hocking, whose personal best on the 500 MV Agusta was recorded back in 1962. Two places further down is another rider now dead, John Hartle, with a 1963 lap on a 500 Gilera that was virtually the 1957 model dusted down and dressed in a more fashionable fairing. Five years later and less than a second slower came little Bill Ivy, whose death soon after compounded yet another tragedy: the most astonishing feat of his career was to complete a 100.32 mph lap of the Island in 1968 on a 125 Yamaha, but during the same week he logged a 250 lap that puts him in thirteenth place by today's absolute standards. Those Yamahas were incredible machines, complex to maintain and tune, fearsome to contemplate, and extremely demanding to ride, water-cooled disc-valved twin-crankshaft two-strokes mustering something like 300 bhp per litre. Yet if that thirteenth place in history's listings seems extraordinary, consider the places above it: five of the fastest nine men around the Island were mounted on a simple two-cylinder Yamaha clearly and closely related to the 350 roadster that is freely available for anybody to buy.

The Yamaha twin must be one of the greatest classics of all time, an over-the-counter giant-killer. The racing two-stroke, based so frankly on the road-going motorcycles bearing the same badge of crossed tuning forks, proved so blisteringly fast and so manageable that the 250 and 350 classes are, after seven years, still completely dominated by it. At club level there are special non-Yamaha races to give the others a chance: even at international level there are circuits where a 350 Yamaha is still faster than anything else regardless of size or power. It is not all that long since even the Daytona 200, a race as fast and furious as any, was almost a foregone conclusion in the 350 Yamaha's favour despite opposition from all the highly-reputed blasters boasting twice as much engine.

Manufacturers of some of the world's finest musical instruments (which explains the tuning forks emblem), Yamaha went into the motor vehicle business in 1955 with a capital of about £30,000. Within ten years their capital was more like a million, and they were building more than 13,000 motorcycles a month. After another ten years, nobody would bother to estimate their standing in terms of mere figures: the reputation of their motorcycles on road and track is too transcendental to be calculated by mere accountants. Likewise there is more for the philosopher than for the technician in the thought that, after reaching such heights of sophistication with the micro-cylindered disc-valve racers of 1968, they should have reverted to simple piston-controlled parallel-twin two-strokes which basically are what they began racing with in 1961.

In the chicken-wired glamour of the Daytona Speedway, leading American riders ready their Yamahas for the annual 200-miler that has become – like the Yamaha itself – a modern classic.

That was the year in which the fates prompted Ernst Degner to leave MZ, to forswear life in a controlled economy, and to put his two-stroke technology (acquired at the elbow of Walter Kaaden) at the disposal of the two-stroke makers of Hamamatsu: first Suzuki and then Yamaha latched gratefully onto the concepts and formulae that Degner brought with him, and once they had applied the research and development facilities that MZ would so dearly have liked, there was no stopping them. Racing two-strokes improved at a rate that was positively alarming: as their specific power outputs grew higher and higher, their rev-bands grew narrower and narrower, their gearboxes needed more and more ratios, their carburation and mechanical efficiency were dependent on every whim of temperature and weather – even though the water-cooling solved the worst of the problems – and their ignition difficulties demanded solutions that the electronics industry was not to perfect for some years to come. It was dizzy, but it was a kind of progress – and it was therefore something at which the old gentlemen of the FIM, the governing body of international motorcycle racing, looked askance.

Whatever their true reasons, and whatever their pretexts, they decided to restrict 125 and 250 cc racers to two-cylinder engines and six-speed gearboxes. Yamaha's reaction was to recognize the promotional possibilities inherent in developing a racer on the basis of their production roadsters, a decision they can never have regretted. Over the ensuing years, both roadsters and racers changed: the number of ports in the cylinder walls gradually increased, the

BELOW RIGHT One year's Yamaha racer is superficially the same as another's. This one dates from 1972, but little more than the brakes and the cooling will be seen to change.

BELOW Privateer's pit-stop, Le Mans 1966.

effective working range of the engine has been widened (notably by the introduction of reed valves downstream of the carburettors), drum brakes have
given way to discs, frames and steering geometry have been altered with
monotonous regularity and modest effect. In some things at least the racers are
significantly different: they are water-cooled, most of the really quick ones
have Dresda rear forks, all of them are frantically noisy and extremely thirsty,
and they would look as strange without their fairings as a roadster would with
one. Nevertheless they are indubitably the most successful motorcycles in
racing, clearly blessed with as much engine power as their chassis can handle,
and as much road-holding and handling finesse as their speed can justify.
The lesson has been given often enough in the past: too much power is as
bad as too little, and there is no substitute for the ability to stay on the road.

Where Japanese technology would have taken us, had the FIM allowed it,
can only be a matter for idle speculation. Where it has brought us, despite or
because of those blinkered legislators, is something at which we can marvel.
If it was Degner's lot to inaugurate a spectacular digression, it was his hosts
who recognized and reverted to the path along which they could make a possibly
more worthwhile progression. If and when they are finally turned aside by
posterity and perhaps the Clean Air Acts, it is unlikely that any successor to
the Yamaha twin will ever prompt us to marvel as we do at such pure and
almost Hussite simplicity.

BELOW One of the very fastest yet, the
four-cylinder 750 Yamaha works racer.

ABOVE Gathering in the fourteenth world championship of his fabulous career, Giacomo Agostini on the works 350 Yamaha in the 1974 Yugoslavian Grand Prix.

RIGHT David Degens (facing the camera) and Mike Duff (sideways) with a works RD56 Yamaha, looking rather more intriguing without its fairing.

Honda CB750

Ninety-two years after Otto created the motive cycle, Honda created the emotive cycle. When the CB750 appeared late in 1968, everybody was agreed that it was fantastic.

In at least one sense it was surely fantastic, corresponding with the fantasies that many a keen rider had woven in daydreams, ever since the palmy days of the 1950s when the Gilera fours were with magnificent disdain outpacing everything else in racing. For all their light-flywheeled ferocity at Grand Prix speeds, the racing Gileras were quite flexible: their mechanics had been known to use them for urgent shopping trips, keeping them off the cam in towns. This was obviously the recipe for a practical town-and-country road machine; but the illusion began to fade when Honda started to take over the role of habitual victor in racing, with little 250 cc fours that revved beyond 14,000 and could not conceivably be ridden anywhere but on the track. Before long the dream seemed lost: the cylinder quota went up to six, and even the 125 cc racer had five, piling improbability upon extravagance. Yet the rumour persisted that Honda were to produce a roadster four, and when it appeared there was hardly a dreamer who did not recognize the *idée fixe* of his fantasies.

Fantastic? Four carburettors, four cylinders, four exhaust pipes, four reversed-cone megaphone silencers, four gallons of petrol and who could not perform fantastic feats? Not every part came in even numbers: there was 1 overhead camshaft, there were 5 speeds in the gearbox, 15 tools in the kit, 95 octanes would do for the petrol, and there had to be 101 reasons why this ought to be the best motorcycle in quantity production anywhere in the world. From the *frou-frou* rustle of the engine as it idled, to the intense sound spectra that issued from the tail as the revs rose into the 8000s, was a gamut the mere technical specification could fill, quite apart from the sensations of riding the thing. Within a year, evidence piled up to suggest that the thing could be ridden to some purpose: Honda 750 fours won the 24-hour race at Le Mans for the Bol d'Or and the 200 miles race at Daytona. This just heightened the excitement, though we knew that the so-called production racers were no more like the regular over-the-counter jobs than those of any other make. At Daytona the CR750 gave 92 bhp instead of 67, the main castings were in Elektron (as were even the four carburettors), the forks were special, and the whole thing, weighing 85 lb less than the production version, had twice as many big hydraulic front discs to stop it.

The customers at the counter were not going to complain at a mere 67 bhp, a hulking 485 lb, and one huge front disc. Who could be anything but delighted with such an offer when for the best part of a year the Honda fours were in such short supply and great demand that there was actually a black market in them, with people cheerfully handing over sums of money greatly in excess of the listed price, in order to get one?

Tell them that they are dull,
And bid them own that thou art beautiful . . .

Honda's Daytona special, the CR750 four, is wheeled out onto the famous Florida track.

Give or take 150 years, Shelley might have used those lines of his to better purpose in an ode to the Honda four than in his *Epipsychidion*. In 1969 when it began to appear in customer's hands, the CB 750 had rivals that were as fast, as expensive, as well made, as big, and so on; but none of them could match the Honda on all counts, and those that threatened *did* look dull. None could match the combination of speed, style, and a feline air of latent ferocity that made the Honda a most exciting and yet relaxing machine; nor were they as beautiful.

The mere possession of four cylinders does not guarantee beauty: look at the old Henderson, the Squariel, or the V-4 Brough Superior. Neither do frames and forks and chromium flashes: great heavens, motorcycles have scarcely varied in these since motorcycling began, with the salutary exception of Neracher's 1922 Neracar which was reputed to steer better than anything made before or since. Details, however, and the harmonious balancing of components, can make a world of difference, and the detail work on the Honda four looked delicious. It was by no means cheap, and lower standards would have been unacceptable.

You got a lot of bike for your money. The Honda was higher, heavier, and longer, than most others, and shortness of leg was as effective a disqualification from ownership as shortness of money. Once on the move it ceased to be so big, for it was nicely balanced and steered with the sort of accuracy expected of well-bred middleweights. Only the sit-up-and-beg riding posture, dictated by the fashion leaders of California who were brought up on Harley Davidsons and therefore knew no better – but who had enough money to qualify them as the most important market in the world – hindered the comfortable realization of all the performance at the Honda's disposal. The usual solution of the quandary created by wind pressure threatening to tear the rider off and cast him adrift at three-figure speeds is to lie down instead of sitting up; but to do so was difficult with those high ear-scratcher handlebars. Factory graphs of resistance and tractive effort showed the prone rider's maximum speed to be 125 mph in neutral conditions. Very likely; the way it accelerated when top gear was engaged at just 100, with 6700 rpm on the rev counter and the torque building up to its peak at 7000, one could readily have been persuaded that 130 was possible.

What seemed to matter to most riders was the performance at the other end of the scale. The 750's low-speed acceleration was tremendous, though reputedly there were other lighter if less powerful machines that could rival it. What they lacked was the ability to keep pace with the Honda as gear succeeded gear, as traffic light sprints and urban limits were left behind: the CB 750 accelerated hard all the way.

It could also go slowly. The engine was so flexible that top gear could be held down to 1000 rpm, which was practically tick-over speed. Even if it stalled, which was unlikely, a little tweak of the twistgrip and a jab of the starter button sent the heavily damped revcounter needle scurrying around the dial again, trying to keep pace with the engine. Starting a motorcycle had lost all its terrors.

Stopping the Honda was another revelation. It was a heavy motorcycle, but the front brake was a huge disc nearly a foot in diameter, its pads hydraulically clamped to produce stopping power quite capable of dealing with greater and faster-moving masses than this. The trouble was that it needed a lot of muscle on the lever – an unattractive prospect when the fear of locking the front wheel through trying a bit too hard is one of the strongest inhibitions a rider can know. Yet it was not the stopping nor the starting, but the manner of the machine's going, that made the CB 750 inimitable. Here was as much performance as you needed, almost as much as you could want, and a docility that would be commendable in something half as fast and twice as energy-consuming.

The whole character of this Honda was summarized in the noise it made. There was none of the spasmodic eructation of large cylinders in small numbers which pound their furious mortars in a sequence of jerk, heave, and bellow; not any such dull opiate as the two-stroke's shallow whine, or the toothless mumblings and borborigmal mutterings of a pushrod engine in touring tune. The Honda had in its registration the peal of trumpets, the noble range of the full diapason, and the subtlety of *vox humana* – and they were for the rider alone to enjoy and interpret, falling so richly upon no ears but his. For some curious reason (perhaps because it departed so rapidly from earshot) the big four made little aural impression on the bystander, even when the throttles were opened to sate the rider's ears with their harmonic-laden glee. To the one *Gewitter*, to the other *Ausbruch* – the lightning flies as fast, only the onomatopoeia is changed for the benefit of the piper-payer.

And if the tune thus called suggested a degree of engine tune bordering on

PREVIOUS PAGES
LEFT It looks almost standard; apart from the tummy pad, dropped handlebars and unsilenced unfiltered carburettor intakes, this CB750 Honda may well be as standard as it looks, for early riders never felt that it lacked performance.
RIGHT The 1971 works 750 racer, seen here Goodyear-tyred for Daytona, was far less standard than it looked.

the improbabilities of the Grand Prix racing in which Honda fours of earlier years were so dominant, there was something else to ponder. Where, but in the Honda or a Wankel, would you associate in 1969 a 9-to-1 compression ratio and well over 8000 rpm with cheap three-star petrol? It was easy to dismiss the CB 750 as a racing engine gone wrong: it was fairer to welcome it as a touring heavyweight made right.

Lamentably, the passing of the years and the passing of the Clean Air Acts and kindred pieces of political expediency enforced a deterioration that was no less lamentable for passing unnoticed by so many customers. The power and speed diminished, the weight and consumption increased, and although the Honda's few solecisms of handling were gradually eradicated (trimmer handlebars alone made a big improvement) the results no longer seemed fantastic. Of course races were still won by Honda-engined bikes, but they were compounded of race-bred chassis by Dresda or Egli, and hyper-ventilated engines by Japauto or Yoshimura, engines enlarged to 810, 910, 960, or even more than 1000 cc and quite capable of delivering more than 100 bhp; but nobody saw any relevance to the standard CB 750 in its increasingly bronchitic state of health. Only after half a dozen years of decline did Honda stop the rot with a new range of 750 fours, in which there was an unabashed tourer for those whose doctrine was *suaviter in modo*, and an avowedly sporting CB 750F for those who preferred *fortiter in re*. Thus revived, the Honda offered again, as at its outset, a combination of performance and price, such a glamorous piece of popular engineering, as had been beyond an enthusiast's wildest dreams until they were made real with this, the greatest and most enduring of the superbikes. It has toured around the world, raced up quarter-mile strips or through 24-hour stretches, carried policemen and pop idols, and created a lifestyle for which the world's motorcycle industry must be profoundly grateful. If any one bike could be held responsible for the motorcycling revival of the 1970s, it was the 750 four.

Longer and lower, rebraked and resprung, repiped and revised, the 1976 CB750F has recovered all the lost power of the original 750 Honda and now has the handling to suit its performance.

Kawasaki Z1

'Power corrupts; lack of power corrupts absolutely.' The dictum of Lord Acton may be more famous, but this parody of it by Adlai Stevenson is more telling – not least to the superbike rider, whether he feel contempt or compassion for the pilots of the tiddlers and mopeds that parade their disturbing humility on the roads of which his mount makes him master. Lack of power makes a motorcycle fatuous, embarrassing and dangerous, but it is a lack that no Kawasaki on the road ever need suffer. After the best part of a century of trying hard, since Shozo Kawasaki founded a dockyard in Tokyo, Kawasaki Heavy Industries are big and powerful, versed in the technology of locomotives, supertankers, aircraft and what not; and when they created a Motorcycle Division in 1968, they envisaged products that would in their own way be big and powerful.

What they did not envisage was that the highly refined four-cylinder four-stroke that they had planned was also a design objective of Honda, a firm then nearly twenty years old and with nearly ten million motorcycles already built. Even before the Kawasaki motorcycle division was formed, key designers had schemed a 750 cc engine; but the public announcement of the CB 750 Honda sent them scurrying back to shelter. A review of their objectives showed that the Kawasaki motorcycle, when it appeared, would have to be bigger and better than the Honda, and practical trials of their rival soon showed that although making a bigger one might not be difficult, making a better one would be far from easy. Time was not necessarily against them: Honda's lead could be exploited for, as the first of a new generation of elaborate high-power roadsters, and one for which long-term success seemed assured, it could be left the unwelcome task of breaking the commercial ice, of finding and capturing a market that could then be relatively easily seduced by Kawasaki when they were good and ready. In the meantime a diversion – or was it a counter-irritant? – was necessary, and it did not take long to produce one. The three-cylinder H1 Kawasaki, marketed as the Mach 3, was a more or less dirigible fire-cracker with a perpetually short fuse, an incorrigible and intemperate half-litre two-stroke that instilled respect among onlookers and put the fear of God into its riders.

Once this line of two-strokes had been started, and for that matter extrapolated down into morphologically similar threes of rather smaller capacity and even greater thirst, there was no incentive to stop their production when eventually Kawasaki were ready with the mild-mannered four-stroke that was the most powerful (and in some circumstances the most abstemious) of them all.

In fact when Kawasaki introduced their four-stroke four-cylinder Z1 model in 1973 they were not ready for the tremendous impact it made upon the motorcycle world. That world was not ready for the Z1 either, flabbergasted to find that its engine displacement was no less than 903 cc, incredulous when inspection proved that from its double overhead camshafts to its elaborate built-up crankshaft, and taking into account all the effulgent furniture between,

Savoyard Georges Godier on the Egli-framed Kawasaki long–distance racer at Thruxton in 1974.

BELOW For 24-hour races such as the Bol d'Or, the Franco–Swiss team of Godier and Genoud were outstandingly successful with this so-called Kawasaki, within the purpose-built chassis of which only the four-cylinder engine and transmission were of Japanese provenance.

FAR LEFT First and most furious of the superfast Kawasakis was the three-cylinder 500 two-stroke, from which was derived the prodigiously fast H2R 750 ridden here by Gary Nixon.

LEFT The 750 Green Meanie in European trim, ridden by Barry Ditchburn at Silverstone in 1975.

the Z1 was not only clearly meant to outdo Honda, but at least in some respects had succeeded. The Z1 was an instant success, so much so that the Kawasaki factory in Akashi was at first embarrassed by the heavy demand. The machine had been under development, with riders hammering it privily across America as well as around Japan, since 1967; but not until 1973 was well under way did a new engine factory come on stream to increase the flow of production and diminish the turbulence of impatient customers.

Whatever the discrepancy between supply and demand, the Kawasaki publicity machine did not hesitate to promote this extravagant machine in a fittingly extravagant way. Soon motorcycling journalists all over America and Europe were unleashing torrents of superlatives with which to convey their astonished admiration of the Z1 in general and of its engine in particular. In this particular, their superlatives were amply justified: the engine was rated at no less than 82 bhp at 8500 rpm, but its exemplary mechanical smoothness was backed by an astonishing flexibility and lack of temperament. There was power available at tick-over speed, power that became simply and steplessly more almighty as the revolutions rose. The gearbox was a five-speeder, with top gear high enough to have true overdrive characteristics; yet the engine was so grandiloquent in torque that the machine could be ridden quite purposefully in town traffic in that same top gear. With such a superfluity of urge, the performance was at once sensational and predictable, with a maximum speed of about 132 mph and acceleration such as would encompass a standing quarter mile in $12\frac{1}{2}$ seconds. Its strength was ferocious, yet this was the most civilized engine ever to propel a motorcycle. Its four silencers kept the exhaust noise down to a whisper most of the time, suffering it to rise only to a hollow baritone moan when the four throttles were open and the revs were high. A positive crankcase ventilation system reduced pollution by recycling blow-by gases and thus minimizing hydrocarbon emissions, while specially hardened sintered-alloy valve seats allowed the use of lead-free petrol, so that the exhaust would be even more sanitary. Add to this the fact that the relatively low compression ratio allowed the burning of cheap low-grade fuel, and the ambivalence of this paralyzingly powerful and apologetically innocuous engine became even more extraordinary.

Inevitably there were special stunts staged to give the propaganda extra impact. A fairly standard Z1, admittedly very carefully prepared but modified only in the handlebars and riding position, the removal of indicators and replacement of the rear suspension units, ran for 24 hours around the Daytona speedway at an average speed of 109.64 mph, including fuel stops and maintenance checks. This was admittedly only 0.36% better than the R69S BMW had achieved around the Montlhery bowl back in 1961; but the BMW was much more comprehensively modified, especially in the engine. In the high temperatures prevailing in Florida, the Kawasaki demonstration was one of convincing reliability. What could be done when the engine was modified was shown at the same track at about the same time: a Z1 with the engine tuned to deliver more than 100 bhp set a new 160.28 mph record, which left no one in any doubt about the progress made in a dozen years.

Impressive as these demonstrations were, they were not entirely convincing

ABOVE The original roadgoing 500 three was christened the Mach 3; it looked like a rush job and went like one.

OPPOSITE
The 900 four-cylinder four-stroke Kawasaki Z1 was a hush job that took the world by storm when it was finally released.
INSET Winners of the 1974 Thruxton 500, Ballington and Ditchburn flank Stan Shenton, entrant of their Kawasaki 750.

because the banking of the Daytona speed bowl made them tantamount to straight-line operations. It was nice to know that the Z1 was directionally stable at high speeds, but there is more to the high-performance motorcycle than that. The journalists had been a little mealy-mouthed about the Kawasaki's handling, which was not at all bad at ordinary speeds but grew unmanageable if the rider attempted to use all the available performance on devious roads. Only gradually did the realization also dawn that the Z1 was very sensitive to tyres: the Japanese Dunlop at the front was specially designed for it, and attempts to substitute something with more wet-weather grip than Japanese tyres were then able to muster generally foundered in a storm of bad handling and language to match. Finally there was some dissatisfaction with the braking: the huge single disc at the front was quite effective at high speeds but hard work when going more slowly, yet it was not until late in 1975 that the arduous task of arresting this high-speed 500-pounder was eased by duplication of the disc.

Despite all this, Kawasaki were able to advertise competition successes galore – but while the engine was undoubtedly a winner, it seldom achieved much in the standard frame. In featherbed chassis related to the Dresda, or slung beneath the large-diameter spinal tube of an Egli skeleton, the Z1 was immensely successful in long-distance racing, notably in the hands of the French-Swiss pair Georges Godier and Alain Genoud who completely dominated the Coupe d'Endurance in the European seasons of 1973 and 1974, at venues as different and as difficult as Barcelona, Spa, and Le Mans. For the 1975 season they acquired an even more special chassis, much of which was based on space-frame concepts of triangulation, especially in the critical area around and behind the steering head and in the cantilever-sprung rear forks. The design of this frame was masterminded by Pierre Doncque and Michel Lambert, university lecturers in engineering and design, in consultation with the riders who knew from their experience that rapidity of pit-stops was of crucial importance in long-distance racing. In the 1975 Bol d'Or one of the Kawasaki riders came in after only 2 of the 24 hours had passed, having dropped the plot. The fairing was smashed, the lights and footrests badly damaged, and the engine was firing on only two cylinders. Two of the machine's three mechanics attacked the aircraft fasteners securing the fairing, while the other jerked open the two rubber fasteners that secured the complete tank and seat assembly with its integral battery and electricity centre. New complete units, hanging on the pit walls amid a rich profusion of costly spares, were clipped into place as quickly as the original ones had been ripped off. The machine was out again within two minutes. . . .

Godier and Genoud won the 1975 Bol d'Or almost as conclusively as they had in 1974, and the factory's advertising people made no bones about treating it as a Kawasaki victory, like all the others. But, like so many of the others in Europe's long-distance races, the Z1 seemed to amount to little more than a big-name power-plant and transmission in a special bicycle. Did this confirm the suspicion that the Kawasaki 900 was the world's best engine in one of the world's second-rate chassis? Can we prize the jewel regardless of its setting?

ABOVE David Degens showing all his great skill and ability aboard a Honda-engined Dresda.

LEFT Degens astride the detuned Triumph-engined Dresda on which he won the 24-hour Barcelona race of 1965.

Dresda

'Orthodoxy is my doxy', explained Bishop Warburton, 'Heterodoxy is another man's doxy.' Considering how little fundamental change there has been in the motorcycle as we have known it for three-quarters of a century, orthodoxy must be a faith to which the majority of riders cling religiously. To listen to them, however, apostasy is never very far away: there is always the temptation to daydream about some unorthodox machine, some latter-day Scott or Neracar, that might free us from our slavery to convention, liberate us from the shackles of unreliable road-holding, clumsy handling, pusillanimous brakes, and all the other static and dynamic inadequacies of the standard rule-of-thumb bicycle. Some day motorcycling may celebrate the coming of its own Messiah, a designer who will redeem us from all the sins of seventy-five years commission and omission. Some days it all seems unnecessary, when we bestride some machine that, though formed in much the same image as all the others, nevertheless seems inspired by an altogether greater spirit.

The Dresda is just such a motorcycle, one of those ideal machines that transcend means to become ends in themselves, things to be relished for their own sakes. Astride one, with a blare in the ears and a blur in the eyes and Newton's laws in the crook of the fingers, is to be absorbed in an ecstasy of motion. It is not mere transportation, it is sheer transport; riding it is an almost hallucinatory experience because the motion is achieved extraneously, with the rider virtually immobile. Effecting this peculiar paradox, his toes might twitch an inch for a split-instant gearchange; two fingers of his right hand might curl a little to caress those double-disc front brakes that can so summarily nullify all the speed that the stupendous engine can engender; a quarter turn of the twistgrip will summon again all the urge that the four cylinders can apply to the equally summary nullification of time and distance. Otherwise the rider can remain motionless, a two-wheeled centaur whose every desire is communicated by mere hints of pressure or relaxation at the controls. The rider thinks; the machine moves. All motorcycles should be like this. What other road-going motorcycles are?

The Dresda is a road-going motorcycle, one that can be ridden with perfect legality on the public highway. It is also a racer, bred in the longest and most strenuous of European production machine events. In its most highly developed form, and geared for tight and twisty tracks such as the Montjuich Park venue for the Barcelona 24-hour race, or the Bugatti circuit at Le Mans for the equally long Bol d'Or, it does about 145 mph; with sprockets changed to suit the long fast stretches of Spa and Mettet, Dresda's youthful proprietor David Degens has ridden it at 170. Not surprisingly he and his machines have often been the fastest in these events, and there are piles of French and Spanish trophies in his office to prove it.

It was as a short-circuit scratcher in the hard school of British racing that Degens first made his mark. It was in the early 1960s that he began, and in a surprisingly short time he demonstrated a rare combination of flair, courage

ABOVE Low, light, and incredibly controllable, the Triumph-engined Dresda grew out of the 1960s fashion for 650 Tritons.

and intelligence that enabled him to rub shoulders with established stars on the track. The greatest of accolades was nearly his, for he was tested and short-listed for the Honda works team. Fate looked askance on this village Hampden, however, whose lot forbade that he should race in quest of a Grand Prix championship. Circumscribed by ill-fortune so that he could not continue in racing, he had to cultivate the little motorcycle business he had acquired; and under its title, Dresda Autos, he developed a reputation as maker of some of the most satisfactory Tritons then being built.

The Triton was a peculiarly English compromise, a hallowing of established orthodoxies. In the engines of road-going motorcycles there was then nothing to compare for availability, unburstability, and power, with the 650 Triumph twin: nor was any chassis considered the peer of the Norton Dominator featherbed. What was more obvious, then, than to put the Triumph engine in the Norton frame, and to call the result a Triton? To make one was nobody's prerogative: all manner of scruffy monstrosities appeared from backyard work-shops all over the country, some of them good, some of them unbelievably inept, but all boasting the same Attic title, and betraying the same back-basement technology. Degens, with racing experience and native shrewdness his to command, went one better: he dispensed with the Norton chassis, substituting one of his own devising that was better adapted to the purpose, unhampered by the touring-machine conventions that distinguished a production Norton from the street-legal pseudo-racer that the sporting bloods of British motorcycling sought.

He had lost the taste for racing, and his heart has probably never really been in it ever since: when he donned his leathers again, it was not to prove himself but to prove his machinery. For all its speed, it was the reliability of the Dresda that had to be its strong suit. The rider must be able to rely on it implicitly to go and to stop and to steer as well as any motorcycle could, and to keep on doing it. In 1965 he fitted his Dresda with a 650 Triumph engine de-tuned for reliability, with only one carburettor in place of the two that were considered *de rigueur*, and on it he won the 1965 Barcelona 24-hour race, beating all the others by out-cornering them, by out-braking them, and by simply keeping going.

Later he turned to other engines for power to add to the Dresda's predict-ability: the Suzuki 500 twin was the first, in an utterly delicious confection that weighed a trifling 302 lb and was full of detail felicities (such as the feather-weight and fully adjustable linkage for the four cams of the prodigious front brake) that were beyond the wit of most customers to appreciate. Ingenuity and intelligence were everywhere: Ford Cortina taper-roller bearings lent an incorruptible accuracy to the motions of the steering and of the exceptionally distortion-resistant rear fork, while T45 steel and a special BOC brazing material invested the frame with an integrity that it had not occurred to other manufac-turers to seek.

As the fashion for self-starters took hold, the Suzuki twin was supplanted by other engines, including the three-cylinder Suzuki 750; but the one that was to become the classic and almost the definitive Dresda motor was the 750 Honda. For the ordinary rider content with about 130 mph and the safest roadholding of any road-going two-sheeler in the world, the Honda engine could remain in absolutely standard form; for the one who wanted to go faster, or perhaps to race, it could be enlarged and enraged by all the artifices in the tuner's repertoire.

Here was the basis of a machine that could win 24-hour races at sprint speeds, a machine weighing a full hundredweight less than the CB750 out of the Honda crate, a machine with outstanding handling, phenomenal performance, and a past winner's heritage. Japauto, a French company specializing in tuned Hondas and not without their own Bol d'Or experience, recognized the possibilities in the Dresda, and when they set the French 250 and 350 road-racing champion Christian Bourgeois on one in the Le Mans 6-hour race, he found that he could keep up with the out-and-out magnesium-and-shrapnel CR750 racers that Honda had themselves built specially for the Daytona race. It was a good augury: in the 1972 Bol d'Or, the Japauto Dresda cruised through the 24 hours to win easily, and similar Dresdas have been among the doughtiest competitors there in subsequent years.

Most of Degens' business nowadays is in bits and pieces – swinging arms, special exhaust systems, frame kits to which some disaffected or accidented Honda owner can fit his own engine, wheels and front suspension – but occasionally he gets an order for the full specification Dresda Honda, a machine that is built by hand and developed by bottom to offer the quintessence of motorcycling ecstasy, a literally sensational machine which gives a new meaning to immediacy of sensation. Here demand and response are simultaneous: the machine seems to have no inertia at all. Inertia is what makes other bikes merely gather speed, whereas the Dresda just leaps forward. Inertia requires them to be wrestled from bank to bank in an s-bend, where the Dresda flicks right and left like a metronome. Inertia keeps them going when the brakes are squeezed hard, but this Dresda has more stopping power and less mass than any road machine of remotely comparable performance. Such weight as it has is in the right places and earning its keep: the aluminium alloy wheels might look like castings left over from the age of steam, but they are stronger and stiffer and more durable than any conventional confection of rolled strip and wire. The rear fork looks more massive than others but it holds the wheel straight in defiance of the monumental tractive and braking forces that seek to twist it out of alignment. The twin headlamps, flanking the fairing that houses a radiator for the gallon of engine oil pumped through the chassis tubes, serve adequate notice of a corner approaching at Spa speeds. The positivity of every control, the firm location of the rider in a purposefully competent forward lean, all combine to rob fast riding of most of its customary physical sensations, leaving it a matter for almost purely intellectual appreciation.

By this I do not mean dull cerebration; riding the Dresda is more ecstatic than that, a process of mechanical enrichment of the mind with a feedback that would normally be intercepted and traduced by the body on any more common and more slothful machine. An ecstasy of motion, did I say? A distillation of motion, rather, with emotion the outcome.

Suzuki RE5

The Wankel has come a long way since that tiny supercharger inside Gustav Baumm's Flying Hammock was turned inside out to become the wonder engine of the 1960s. Suzuki too have come a long way since Ernst Degner joined them from MZ and set them on an enormously successful course as makers of some of the most persuasive two-stroke motorcycles in the world. Now it has all come together, with Suzuki's own Wankel engine in a motorcycle garnished with equipment as sophisticated as any to be seen on the latest two-wheelers – but although 'sophisticated' is exactly the word for it, it is one that has pejorative undertones. What then are we to make of this convergence of technologies? Is it a pointer to the future, and is that future to be welcomed? We can never know until we experience it whether the future will be to our taste. Whether the RE5 Suzuki appeals to a rider's taste is likewise not to be deduced from looking into it, but only from riding it. Imagine a hefty old-fashioned big single, a heavy-flywheeled and gentle-cammed engine happy to pull like steam from revolutions so low that you can feel every individual plonk of the piston, accompanied by one of those chortling *basso ostinato* exhausts that went out of fashion with bowler hats. You must have in mind a big beefy but tractable machine; and you must expect it to surprise you. It starts with a button, runs without a tremor, and as the revs wind perfectly smoothly into the 5000s it somehow gathers up its skirts and takes off like a racer coming on to the megaphone.

Not, you might think, a bad recipe for an all-round motorcycle. Not, provided it steered and handled and stopped, a bike that could fail to do well on

ABOVE Perhaps cleverer in the engineering than in the marketing, Suzuki's RE5.

LEFT The car-type carburettor is on the left, behind the radiator.

LEFT In roadster and racer forms, the Suzuki 750 two-stroke is impressive – never more so than when Sheene races it, as at Silverstone in 1975.

the market. Not, given reasonable price and quality, a bike to which anyone could object. No? The Wankel-engined Suzuki does have all these characteristics, and it does steer and handle and stop in a style calculated to appeal to many riders and to upset comparatively few, and its price and quality are reasonable by the standards of the times. Yet it does inspire reservations.

None of these misgivings is due to the simple fact that the machine has a Wankel engine. No other is better suited to the motorcycle, for the Wankel is vibrationless and light and capable of yielding all the performance required; it is easy to locate in the best place for good weight distribution and convenient transmission layout; it is insensitive to low-grade fuel, whether leaded or not; and for those who concern themselves with the toxicity of exhaust emissions, it is potentially easier to render sanitary than any conventional piston engine. Altogether it must be preferable to the thumping big cylinders that emissions legislation is tending to enforce on the new generation of motorcycles that will probably have *nolens volens* to be four-strokes. There have admittedly been objections to the Wankel concerned with its thirst and durability: valid though these objections may have been in the infancy of the engine, they do not seem to have much substance in the latter 1970s as the Wankel grows better, and its rivals grow worse.

Perhaps the misgivings are aesthetic: it would be fair to describe the RE5 as an honest motorcycle in that all of its flaws are on the surface instead of lurking covertly within a treacherously bland exterior. It is an aggressively and heavily styled machine, extravagantly decked in jazzy snazzy trivia that start with the functionally inexplicable barrel-housing for the instruments, with its transparent lid which flips open when the ignition key is turned, and continuing through the fancywork around the radiator and the space-fiction exhaust pipes, to the spherical flashers and the cylindrical rear light housing. There is plenty of bright paint and plate and polished metal – and, to be fair, a lot of it is attractive and impressive, especially the excellent assembly of twin stainless-steel disc brakes and well-engineered front forks. Forgetting the ear-scratcher handlebars, it all amounts to something that is a matter of taste rather than of efficiency; but perhaps the aesthetic approach went deeper. Could it be that Suzuki deliberately sought to make this look as much like a conventionally engined motorcycle as possible?

Only its lightweight contemporary the DKW-Hercules Wankel motorcycle looks as though it is the embodiment of a different principle. All the others that we have briefly seen – the ingenious air-cooled Norton, the Comotor-engined leviathan from Van Veen, and the long-gestating Yamaha – look like ordinary ones that have been left to cook too long. So it is with the RE5; was it really necessary for the working portion of the engine, the rotor and housing, to be set so high in the frame, making the bicycle feel top-heavy? Was it necessary for the whole machine to feel so big, and for the tank of such a good tourer to be so small?

This Suzuki is emphatically a touring motorcycle. That is the context in which earlier references to its steering and handling and stopping must be read. It can be laid over and cornered fairly hard, though the stand gets in the way on steep left-handers; it can be hauled down from high speeds without too much muscular exertion on the brake levers; its behaviour is always predictable. Its responses are slow, however, and not calculated to appeal to the sporting rider. Going up or down a twisting mountain road, one would ride the RE5 at a comfortable clip without any worries while admiring the air and the scenery; a real rider's machine would prompt you to ignore all that and to concentrate on the sheer motorcycling pleasures of making the actual negotiation of the hill beautiful in its accuracy and fluency of line and speed. A motorcycle is or should be an end in itself, but the RE5 is a means to an end. Whether that should make it more or less of a motorcycle, or for that matter more or less desirable (which is not necessarily the same thing), is something for each individual to decide for himself.

When the conventional yardsticks are applied, the RE5 measures up fairly well. With 62 bhp supposedly at its disposal, it is not unreasonable that the great weight and frontal area of this very upright motorcycle should eventually be overcome to carry the speed to 110 mph. With a five-speed gearbox essentially the same as that of the 750 cc Suzuki three-cylinder two-stroke, and with the same particularly low bottom gear – and an even rougher change into and out of it, perhaps because of the greater flywheel effect in the Wankel engine – it is not surprising that its acceleration is quite respectable too, especially when the engine really comes on song at high rpm. This is a well-known characteristic of Wankel engines with peripheral porting, but it is unusual for them to be as tractable at low speed as this Suzuki is. The secret lies in the carburation, a car-type two-stage Solex instrument supplying two tiny peripheral ports from its primary stage while a big secondary opens communications with a cavernous maw that gapes like the mouths of the bulls of Bashan whenever speed and power are sought. The system is strange to motorcycles, giving flexibility in exchange for responsiveness, and it prompts the same questioning as do so many other items in the RE5 specification: it is clever, but is it good?

'Cleverness is up', says Russell Burlingham in his book on Forrest Reid, 'and if ever any one thing were more certain than the evanescence of all mere cleverness, that something is its popularity today.' Whether in motorcycles or any other commodity, the stylists and marketing men have made it difficult to distinguish between the steak and the sizzle. A Wankel-engined motorcycle ought to be good, but this one defies us to presume it good on the strength of its Wankel engine – yet it alone in its class has been commercially successful. Perhaps, like its petrol consumption (which can vary from an absurd 20 mpg to a tolerable 40 or more), it depends on where and how, and why and by whom, it is ridden.

Where could be almost anywhere, for the machine is perfectly happy in town apart from that unpleasant change from first to second gear, but it is perhaps happiest of all on motorways where high speeds can be sustained with a comfort unknown to any motorcyclist condemned to reciprocating engines. *How* it is ridden, bearing in mind the predictable but ponderous responses of this heavyweight, will depend more than usually on where it is ridden. *Why* it should be ridden and *by whom* is another matter entirely, one which must ultimately be a matter of taste. Perhaps we should allow the future to supply an arbiter.

Fastest 500 yet, the four-cylinder two-stroke Suzuki.

OVERLEAF
The Suzuki RE5.

153

Acknowledgments

The illustrations in this book are reproduced by kind permission of the following agencies and individuals. Numbers refer to pages.

2–3 author
6 M. Carling
10–11 Michelin Co. Ltd
12 David Burgess-Wise
13 Eric Osborne
14 above National Motor Museum
14 below David Burgess-Wise
15 left and right, 16, 17, 18–19, 20–21 National Motor Museum
21 Sport and General Press Agency
22–3 Science Museum, London, lent by Mr P. A. Clare
23 Radio Times Hulton Picture Library
24 above National Motor Museum
24 below Radio Times Hulton Picture Library
25 National Motor Museum
26 Rex Features – Fotos International
26–7 National Motor Museum
28–9, 29 right, 30, 30–31, 32 National Motor Museum
29 left Presspix – Syndication International
33 Weidenfeld and Nicolson Archives
34–5, 35 Eric Osborne
38–9 National Motor Museum
40 Press Association
40–41 Eric Osborne
41 National Motor Museum
42–3 Rex Features – Fotos International
44 Syndication International
44–5 National Motor Museum
46–7 Eric Osborne
49 above National Motor Museum
49 below Fox Photos
50–51 Foto-Nicholls
51 Eric Thompson
52 Foto-Nicholls
53, 54, 55 National Motor Museum
56 above and below Popperfoto
58 Associated Press
59 Weidenfeld and Nicolson Archives
60 above Press Association
60 below Keystone Press Agency
61 Associated Press
62 Mick Woollett
64 Press Association
65 above Keystone Press Agency
65 below Museo dell'Automobile, Turin
66–7 Rex Features – Fotos International
67 Roy Harper
68 Radio Times Hulton Picture Library
69 Conway Motors
70–71 Eric Osborne
71 Conway Motors
72 Basil Smith
73 Fox Photos
74, 74–5 Eric Osborne
76 above and below E. F. Brockway, Douglas (Sales and Service) Ltd

78 Mick Woollett
80–81 Press Association (National Motor Museum)
81 Keystone Press Agency
82 Press Association
83 Mick Woollett
84–5 National Motor Museum
85 BMW
86 author
87 Mick Woollett
88 above Deutsches Museum, Munich (National Motor Museum)
88 below BMW
89 Roy Hall
91, 92–3 Bruce Main-Smith
95 Syndication International
96–7 Motorcycle Sport
97 Süddeutscher Verlag, Munich
98 above NSU (National Motor Museum)
98 below Eric Thompson
101 above Manx Press Pictures (National Motor Museum)
101 below Süddeutscher Verlag, Munich
102 Foto-Nicholls
104–5, 105 Weidenfeld and Nicolson Archives
107 above Popperfoto
107 below Weidenfeld and Nicolson Archives
109 above Keystone Press Agency
109 below Gerhard Fuhr, Leipzig
110 Foto-Nicholls
111 Mick Woollett
112–13 Foto-Nicholls
113 Associated Press
114–15 Foto-Nicholls
116–17 Keystone Press Agency
118 above author
118 below Keystone Press Agency
120–21 Weidenfeld and Nicolson Archives
122, 123 above Behram Kapadia
123 below Vajenti Centro Fotografico
124, 125 Weidenfeld and Nicolson Archives
126, 128, 128–9 Mick Woollett
129 author
130 Keystone Press Agency
130–31, 133, 134–5, 135 Mick Woollett
137 Weidenfeld and Nicolson Archives
138–9 Foto-Nicholls
140 above left Mick Woollett
140 above right, 140–41 Keystone Press Agency
142 LBA, Sweden
143 J. H. Norman
143 inset Foto-Nicholls
144, 144–5 Dresda Autos Ltd
146 author
146–7 author
148 Dresda Autos Ltd
150, 150–51 Suzuki (GB) Ltd (Maurice Spalding Publicity)
132 Keystone Press Agency
133 Mick Woollett
154–5 Behram Kapadia
endpapers author

Picture research by Carina Dvorak

Index